Houghton
Mifflin
Harcourt

CALIFORNIA

MATH

Expressions

Common Core

Dr. Karen C. Fuson

GRADE

2

Volume 1

This material is based upon work supported by the
National Science Foundation
under Grant Numbers
ESI-9816320, REC-9806020, and RED-935373.

Any opinions, findings, and conclusions, or recommendations expressed in this material
are those of the author and do not necessarily reflect the views of the National Science Foundation.

VOLUME 1 CONTENTS

UNIT 1 Addition and Subtraction Within 20

BIG IDEA 1	Strategies for Addition and Subtraction

* This lesson consists only of activities from the Teacher Edition.

VOLUME 1 CONTENTS **iii**

© Houghton Mifflin Harcourt Publishing Company

* This lesson consists only of activities from the Teacher Edition.

© Houghton Mifflin Harcourt Publishing Company

Family Letter

Content Overview

Dear Family:

Your child is learning math in a program called *Math Expressions,* which links mathematical ideas to a child's everyday experiences. This helps children understand math better.

In this program, your child will learn math and have fun by

- working with objects and making drawings of math situations.
- listening to and working with other children and sharing ways to solve problems.
- writing and solving problems and connecting math to daily life.
- helping classmates learn.

Your child will have homework almost every day. He or she needs a Homework Helper. The helper may be anyone—a family member, an older brother or sister, a neighbor, or a friend. Set aside a definite time for homework and provide your child with a quiet place to work where there are no distractions. Encourage your child to talk about what is happening in math class. If your child is having problems with math, please talk to me to see how you might help.

Please cut, fill in, and return the bottom part of this letter.

Thank you. You are very important to your child's learning.

Sincerely,
Your child's teacher

 CA CC

Unit 1 addresses the following standards from the *Common Core State Standards for Mathematics with California Additions:* **2.OA.1, 2.OA.2, 2.OA.3, 2.NBT.2, 2.NBT.5, 2.NBT.6, 2.NBT.9,** and all Mathematical Practices.

My child _____ will have
(child's name)

_____ as a Homework Helper.
(name of Homework Helper)

This person is my child's _____ .
(relationship to child)

_____
signature of parent or guardian

Carta a la familia

Un vistazo general al contenido

Estimada familia:

Su niño está aprendiendo matemáticas con un programa llamado *Math Expressions,* que relaciona conceptos matemáticos abstractos con la experiencia diaria de los niños. Esto ayuda a los niños a entender mejor las matemáticas.

Con este programa, su niño va a aprender matemáticas y se divertirá mientras:

- trabaja con objetos y hace dibujos de situaciones matemáticas.
- escucha y trabaja con otros estudiantes y comparte con ellos estrategias para resolver problemas.
- escribe y resuelve problemas, y relaciona las matemáticas con la vida diaria.
- ayuda a sus compañeros de clase a aprender.

Su niño tendrá tarea casi todos los días y necesitará que alguna persona lo ayude. Esa persona puede ser, usted, un hermano mayor, un vecino o un amigo. Establezca una hora para la tarea y ofrezca a su niño un lugar donde trabajar sin distracciones. Anímelo a comentar lo que está aprendiendo en la clase de matemáticas. Si él tiene problemas con las matemáticas, hable por favor con el maestro para ver cómo puede usted ayudar.

Por favor recorte, complete y devuelva el formulario al maestro.

Muchas gracias. Usted es imprescindible en el aprendizaje de su niño.

Atentamente,
El maestro de su niño

 CA CC

En la Unidad 1 se aplican los siguientes estándares auxiliares, contenidos en los *Estándares estatales comunes de matemáticas con adiciones para California*: 2.0A.1, 2.0A.2, 2.0A.3, 2.NBT.2, 2.NBT.5, 2.NBT.6, 2.NBT.9 y todos los de prácticas matemáticas.

- -

La persona que ayudará a mi niño _____ es
　　　　　　　　　　　　　　　　　　(nombre del niño)

_____. Esta persona es
(nombre de la persona)

_____ de mi niño.
(relación con el niño)

_____
　　　　　　　　　　Su firma

© Houghton Mifflin Harcourt Publishing Company

　　　　　　　　　　　　　Represent Addition and Subtraction

▶ Relate Math Mountains and Equations for Addition

$8 + 6 = \boxed{14}$

$10 + 4 = 14$

Discuss the **Math Mountain** and the **equation**.

1. Where is the **total**? Where are the **partners** or **addends**?

2. Tell word problems for both.

3. Solve both and compare your strategies.

▶ Relate Math Mountains and Equations for Subtraction

$9 + \boxed{6} = 15$

$15 - 9 = \boxed{6}$

Discuss this Math Mountain and the equations.

4. Where is the total? Where are the partners or addends?

5. Tell word problems for all.

6. Solve all and compare your strategies.

► Count On for Addition or Subtraction

7. For addition, I pretend I already counted 9. Then I count on 3 more to get the total. I stop when I see/feel 3. I hear 12, the unknown total.

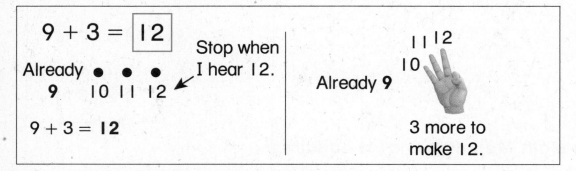

8. For subtraction, I pretend I already counted 9. I count on until I get to 12. I stop when I hear 12. I see/feel 3, the unknown partner.

► Patterns in Equations for Math Mountains

9. Discuss patterns in the eight equations for the Math Mountain with total 12 and partners 9 and 3.

$9 + 3 = 12$ $12 = 9 + 3$

$3 + 9 = 12$ $12 = 3 + 9$

$12 - 9 = 3$ $3 = 12 - 9$

$12 - 3 = 9$ $9 = 12 - 3$

Represent Addition and Subtraction

▶ Write Equations for Math Mountains

10. Write two equations for each Math Mountain.

$9 + 5 =$ ☐ **0**

~~8 + 5~~

$4 + 8 = 12$

$8 + 4 = 12$

$8 + 7 = 15$

▶ Draw Math Mountains

11. Draw a Math Mountain and write one more equation.

$9 + 6 = \boxed{}$

_____

$9 + \boxed{3} = 12$

_____

$8 + \boxed{} = 16$

_____

$5 + 6 = \boxed{}$

_____

$13 - 4 = \boxed{}$

_____

$15 - 7 = \boxed{}$

_____

Represent Addition and Subtraction

Family Letter

Content Overview

Dear Family:

Your child is exploring addition and subtraction equations with Math Mountain Cards. The cards have a large number at the top and two smaller numbers at the bottom. From the cards, children can see that two smaller numbers can be added together to make a larger number. They can also see that a large number can be broken apart into two smaller numbers.

Children will write addition and subtraction equations that they can make from the cards, as shown in the example. The two partners, 9 and 6, can be added to make the total, 15. They can be switched (6 and 9) and still make 15.

$9 + 6 = 15$

$6 + 9 = 15$

$15 - 9 = 6$

$15 - 6 = 9$

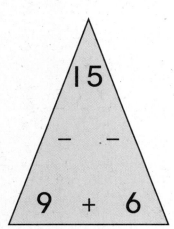

$15 = 9 + 6$

$15 = 6 + 9$

$6 = 15 - 9$

$9 = 15 - 6$

Students see and write all eight equations. It is important for understanding algebra that they sometimes see equations with only one number on the left.

Please call if you need practice materials. Thank you for helping your child learn about the relationship between addition and subtraction.

Sincerely,
Your child's teacher

 CA CC

Unit 1 addresses the following standards from the *Common Core State Standards for Mathematics with California Additions:* **2.0A.1, 2.0A.2, 2.0A.3, 2.NBT.2, 2.NBT.5, 2.NBT.6, 2.NBT.9,** and all Mathematical Practices.

Estimada familia:

Su niño está aprendiendo ecuaciones de suma y resta usando las tarjetas *Math Mountain*. Las tarjetas tienen un número grande en la parte superior y dos números más pequeños en la parte inferior. En las tarjetas los niños pueden ver que se pueden sumar dos números más pequeños para obtener un número más grande. También pueden ver que un número grande se puede separar en dos números más pequeños.

Los niños escribirán ecuaciones de suma y resta que puedan hacer a partir de las tarjetas, según se muestra en el ejemplo. Se pueden sumar las dos partes, 9 y 6, para obtener el total, 15. También se pueden intercambiar (6 y 9) y todavía obtener 15.

$9 + 6 = 15$

$6 + 9 = 15$

$15 - 9 = 6$

$15 - 6 = 9$

$15 = 9 + 6$

$15 = 6 + 9$

$6 = 15 - 9$

$9 = 15 - 6$

15

– –

9 + 6

Los estudiantes ven y escriben las ocho ecuaciones. Para comprender álgebra es importante que vean ecuaciones con un solo número a la izquierda.

Por favor comuníquese conmigo si necesita materiales para practicar. Gracias por ayudar a su niño a aprender la relación entre suma y resta.

Atentamente,
El maestro de su niño

© Houghton Mifflin Harcourt Publishing Company

CA CC

En la Unidad 1 se aplican los siguientes estándares auxiliares, contenidos en los *Estándares estatales comunes de matemáticas con adiciones para California*: **2.OA.1, 2.OA.2, 2.OA.3, 2.NBT.2, 2.NBT.5, 2.NBT.6, 2.NBT.9** y todos los de prácticas matemáticas.

0 + 1   0   2
0 + 3   4
0 + 5   6

1

3

5

0 + 0   0 + 2   0 + 4   0 + 6
0 + 7   0 + 6   1 + 2   1 + 4
8   2   4

7   6   3   5

0 + 8   1 + 1   1 + 3
1 + 9   1 + 8   2 + 2   2 + 2
6   8   10   5

7   6   4

1 + 5   1 + 7   1 + 9   3 + 2
4 + 2   6 + 2   8 + 2   3 + 3
7   9   10

6   8   10   9
5 + 2   7 + 2   5 + 5

© Houghton Mifflin Harcourt Publishing Company

Math Mountain Cards

Math Mountain Cards (addition and subtraction triangle flash cards):

- 7 = 5 + 3
- 9 = 7 + 3
- 10 = 4 + ...
- 8 = 4 + 5
- 8 / 4 + 3 / 6 + 3
- 10 / 3 + 4 / 6 + 4
- 9 / 4 + 4
- 11 = 6 + 3 / 4 + 7
- 12 = 4 + 6 / 5 + 9
- 11 = 6 + ...
- 12 / 8 + 3
- 11 / 4 + 8
- 13 / 9 + 2
- 11
- 12 / 5 + 8 / 9 + 9 / 8 + 6
- 14
- 13
- 15
- 13 = 5 + 7 / 5 + 9
- 12 = 7 + 6
- 14 = 9 + 6
- 15 / 7 + 7 / 6 + 7 / 8 + ...
- 16 / 9 + 8
- 18
- 14 / 8 + 7
- 16 / 8 + 8
- 17 / 9 + 9

Math Mountain Cards

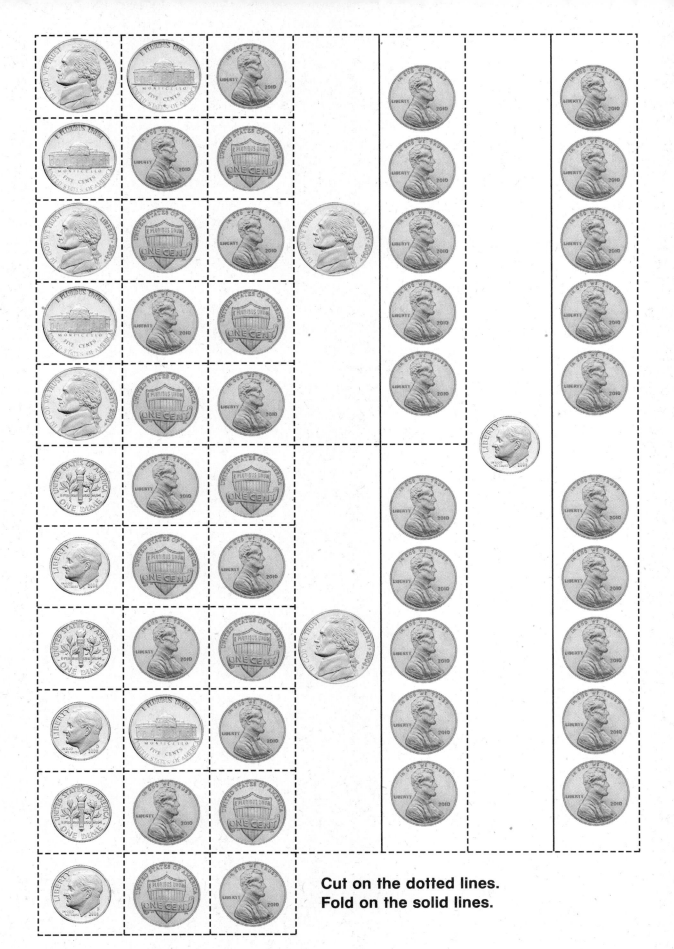

Cut on the dotted lines.
Fold on the solid lines.

Coin Strips **13**

Coin Strips

► Find the Unknown Addend

$7 + \boxed{5} = 12$

10

7 ● ● ● | ● ●

$3 + 2 = 5$

$12 - 7 = \boxed{5}$

● ● ● ● ● ● ● | ● ● ● ● ●

7   5

Find the **unknown addend** (unknown partner).

1. $8 + \boxed{} = 11$ $15 - 6 = \boxed{}$ $8 + \boxed{} = 14$

2. $7 + \boxed{} = 13$ $12 - 8 = \boxed{}$ $3 + \boxed{} = 12$

3. $5 + \boxed{} = 14$ $16 - 9 = \boxed{}$ $9 + \boxed{} = 17$

4. $9 + \boxed{} = 14$ $18 - 9 = \boxed{}$ $7 + \boxed{} = 11$

5. $8 + \boxed{} = 13$ $13 - 9 = \boxed{}$ $15 - \boxed{} = 8$

13   13   15
8 □   9 □   □ 8

6. Find the partner for $11 - 6 = \boxed{}$.

Make a math drawing to show what you did.

Name _____

► Practice Finding Teen Totals and Unknown Addends

Are we looking for a partner or total?
Ring the P or the T for each column.

	P or T ↓		P or T ↓		P or T ↓
1. $5 + 8 = \square$		$7 + \square = 11$		$11 - 9 = \square$	
2. $4 + 8 = \square$		$9 + \square = 17$		$16 - 8 = \square$	
3. $7 + 9 = \square$		$7 + \square = 12$		$13 - 7 = \square$	
4. $5 + 6 = \square$		$8 + \square = 16$		$14 - 7 = \square$	
5. $7 + 6 = \square$		$9 + \square = 13$		$15 - 7 = \square$	
6. $8 + 3 = \square$		$9 + \square = 18$		$14 - 9 = \square$	
7. $8 + 4 = \square$		$6 + \square = 15$		$12 - 5 = \square$	

Relate Unknown Addends and Subtraction

Name _____

CA CC Content Standards 2.OA.3, 2.NBT.2
Mathematical Practices MP.1, MP.3, MP.6, MP.7, MP.8

► **Count by 2s**

1. Loop **pairs** of sleeping bags.

2. Number the sleeping bags from 1 to 50.

3. Count by 2s from 2 to 50.

2, _____, 6, _____, 10, _____, _____, 16, _____, _____,

_____, 24, _____, _____, _____, _____, _____, 36, _____,

_____, _____, _____, _____, _____, 50

VOCABULARY
pattern

▶ **Patterns**

Count by 2s to complete each **pattern**.

4. 6, 8, _____, _____, 14

5. 12, _____, _____, _____, 20

6. 26, _____, _____, _____, _____

7. _____, _____, _____, _____, 50

8. 50, _____, _____, _____, 58

9. 76, _____, _____, _____, _____

▶ **What's the Error?**

2, 4, 6, 8, 12, 14, 16, 18,

22, 24, 26, 28

I counted by 2s to 28. Did I count correctly?

10. Show how to count by 2s from 2 to 28.

2, _____, _____, _____, _____, _____, _____, _____, _____,

_____, _____, _____, _____, 28

VOCABULARY
odd
even

► **Make Pairs**

Draw lines to make pairs.

Ring **odd** or **even**.

11.

odd   even

12.

odd   even

13.

odd   even

14.

odd   even

15.

odd   even

16.

odd   even

17.

odd   even

18.

odd   even

19.

odd   even

20.

odd   even

VOCABULARY
addition doubles

► **Make Equal Groups**

Try to make equal groups.

Ring odd or even.

21. 9

odd   even

22. 6

odd   even

23. 12

odd   even

24. 7

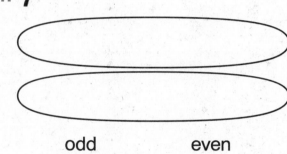

odd   even

► **Write Addition Doubles**

Complete the **addition doubles** equation.

25. $\boxed{} + \boxed{} = 8$

26. $\boxed{} + \boxed{} = 10$

27. $\boxed{} + \boxed{} = 18$

28. $\boxed{} + \boxed{} = 16$

Name _____

CA CC Content Standards **2.0A.2, 2.0A.3**
Mathematical Practices **MP.1, MP.2, MP.8**

VOCABULARY	
addition	subtraction
doubles	doubles
doubles	doubles
plus 1	minus 1
doubles	doubles
plus 2	minus 2

▶ **Use Doubles**

Addition Doubles and **Subtraction Doubles**	**Doubles Plus 1** and **Doubles Minus 1**	**Doubles Plus 2** and **Doubles Minus 2**
1. $5 + 5 =$ ☐ $10 - 5 =$ ☐	$5 + 6 =$ ☐ $5 + 4 =$ ☐	$5 + 7 =$ ☐ $5 + 3 =$ ☐
2. $6 + 6 =$ ☐ $12 - 6 =$ ☐	$6 + 7 =$ ☐ $6 + 5 =$ ☐	$6 + 8 =$ ☐ $6 + 4 =$ ☐
3. $7 + 7 =$ ☐ $14 - 7 =$ ☐	$7 + 8 =$ ☐ $7 + 6 =$ ☐	$7 + 9 =$ ☐ $7 + 5 =$ ☐
4. $8 + 8 =$ ☐ $16 - 8 =$ ☐	$8 + 9 =$ ☐ $8 + 7 =$ ☐	$8 + 10 =$ ☐ $8 + 6 =$ ☐
5. $9 + 9 =$ ☐ $18 - 9 =$ ☐	$9 + 10 =$ ☐ $9 + 8 =$ ☐	$9 + 11 =$ ☐ $9 + 7 =$ ☐

▶ Use Doubles (continued)

Add. Use doubles.

---

6. $9 + 9 =$ ☐ $8 + 6 =$ ☐ $6 + 5 =$ ☐

---

7. $7 + 7 =$ ☐ $7 + 6 =$ ☐ $9 + 11 =$ ☐

---

8. $11 + 9 =$ ☐ $6 + 8 =$ ☐ $6 + 6 =$ ☐

---

9. $7 + 9 =$ ☐ $5 + 5 =$ ☐ $8 + 7 =$ ☐

---

10. $9 + 8 =$ ☐ $5 + 7 =$ ☐ $6 + 4 =$ ☐

---

11. $8 + 8 =$ ☐ $8 + 10 =$ ☐ $9 + 7 =$ ☐

---

12. $5 + 4 =$ ☐ $6 + 7 =$ ☐ $5 + 6 =$ ☐

---

13. $7 + 8 =$ ☐ $8 + 9 =$ ☐ $7 + 5 =$ ☐

Name _____

CA CC Content Standards **2.0A.2**
Mathematical Practices **MP.2, MP.3, MP.6**

VOCABULARY
equation
equation chain

▶ What's the Error?

1. Help Puzzled Penguin.

$$6 + 3 = \boxed{9} - 5$$

Did I make a mistake?

▶ Use Equations to Make an Equation Chain

2. Solve the **equations**.
   If the answer is 8, color the block .

$8 + 9 = \square$	$12 - 6 = \square$	$7 + 5 = \square$
$5 + 3 = \square$	$17 - 9 = \square$	$13 - 5 = \square$
$5 + 4 = \square$	$1 + 7 = \square$	$15 - 8 = \square$
$11 - 3 = \square$	$4 + 4 = \square$	$3 + 8 = \square$
$16 - 8 = \square$	$6 + 6 = \square$	$5 + 7 = \square$

3. Use the blocks you colored to make an **equation chain**.

_____

Name _____

VOCABULARY
vertical form

► **Show Three Ways**

Write the equation, the **vertical form**, and the Math Mountain.

Use a ⬜ to show the unknown number.

4. 8 and 5 make how many?

_____

5. 7 and what number make 15?

_____

6. 18 take away 8 equals what number?

_____

7. 17 minus 8 makes what number?

© Houghton Mifflin Harcourt Publishing Company

Equations, Equation Chains, and Vertical Form

Dive the Deep

CA CC Content Standards 2.OA.2, 2.NBT.5, 2.NBT.6, 2.NBT.9
Mathematical Practices MP.2, MP.3, MP.6, MP.7

$11 - 6 = \boxed{5}$ $12 - \boxed{6} = 6$ $13 - 8 = \boxed{5}$

$12 - 7 = \boxed{5}$ $17 - \boxed{8} = 9$ $15 - 6 = \boxed{9}$

$12 - 9 = \boxed{3}$ $13 - \boxed{5} = 8$ $11 - 9 = \boxed{2}$

$13 - 4 = \boxed{9}$ $14 - \boxed{6} = 8$ $13 - 9 = \boxed{4}$

$11 - 5 = \boxed{6}$ $17 - \boxed{9} = 8$ $15 - 7 = \boxed{8}$

$14 - 9 = \boxed{5}$ $11 - \boxed{8} = 3$ $14 - 8 = \boxed{6}$

$14 - 7 = \boxed{7}$ $12 - \boxed{4} = 8$ $12 - 5 = \boxed{7}$

$16 - 7 = \boxed{9}$ $16 - \boxed{8} = 8$ $11 - 3 = \boxed{8}$

$11 - 7 = \boxed{4}$ $15 - \boxed{7} = 8$ $13 - 6 = \boxed{7}$

$12 - 3 = \boxed{9}$ $16 - \boxed{9} = 7$ $18 - 9 = \boxed{9}$

$13 - 7 = \boxed{6}$ $11 - \boxed{4} = 7$ $12 - 8 = \boxed{4}$

Dive the Deep

11 − 5 = 6

12 − 5 = 7

12 − 3 = 9

13 − 9 = 4

11 − 6 = 5

14 − 5 = 9

14 − 7 = 7

16 − 9 = 7

11 − 4 = 7

12 − 9 = 3

13 − 6 = 7

12 − 6 = 6

17 − 9 = 8

13 − 8 = 5

14 − 8 = 6

17 − 8 = 9

11 − 3 = 8

12 − 8 = 4

16 − 8 = 8

15 − 8 = 7

16 − 7 = 9

11 − 7 = 4

13 − 5 = 8

15 − 9 = 6

11 − 2 = 9

13 − 4 = 9

15 − 8 = 7

14 − 6 = 8

12 − 7 = 5

11 − 8 = 3

13 − 7 = 6

18 − 9 = 9

12 − 4 = 8

Dive the Deep

▶**Find a Sum of 10**

Ring two addends that make ten. Then write the total.

1. $6 + 9 + 1 =$ ☐   2. $5 + 7 + 3 =$ ☐

3. $5 + 9 + 5 =$ ☐   4. $6 + 4 + 7 =$ ☐

5. $4 + 1 + 6 =$ ☐   6. $1 + 9 + 4 =$ ☐

7. $3 + 2 + 8 =$ ☐   8. $3 + 2 + 7 =$ ☐

▶**Add in Any Order**

Write the total.

9. $9 + 3 + 5 =$ ☐   10. $9 + 7 + 2 =$ ☐

11. $8 + 9 + 2 =$ ☐   12. $7 + 8 + 5 =$ ☐

13. $7 + 5 + 2 =$ ☐   14. $7 + 7 + 2 =$ ☐

15. $3 + 9 + 6 =$ ☐   16. $3 + 8 + 2 =$ ☐

Name _____

▶ Add Four Addends

Add in any order. Write the sum.

17. $4 + 4 + 5 + 2 =$ ☐

18. $8 + 8 + 5 + 2 =$ ☐

19. $5 + 5 + 3 + 9 =$ ☐

20. $3 + 6 + 5 + 4 =$ ☐

21. $4 + 8 + 9 + 3 =$ ☐

22. $1 + 8 + 8 + 4 =$ ☐

▶ (PATH to FLUENCY) Add and Subtract Within 20

Add.

23. $6 + 8 =$ _____

24. $9 + 9 =$ _____

25. $7 + 0 =$ _____

26. $\begin{array}{r} 9 \\ + 7 \\ \hline \end{array}$

27. $\begin{array}{r} 8 \\ + 5 \\ \hline \end{array}$

28. $\begin{array}{r} 8 \\ + 2 \\ \hline \end{array}$

29. $\begin{array}{r} 9 \\ + 9 \\ \hline \end{array}$

Subtract.

30. $\begin{array}{r} 15 \\ - 8 \\ \hline \end{array}$

31. $\begin{array}{r} 9 \\ - 7 \\ \hline \end{array}$

32. $\begin{array}{r} 9 \\ - 0 \\ \hline \end{array}$

33. $\begin{array}{r} 12 \\ - 4 \\ \hline \end{array}$

Add Three or Four Addends

Dear Family:

Your child is learning to solve word problems called *Add To* and *Take From* problems. These problems begin with a quantity that is then modified by change—something is added or subtracted—which results in a new quantity.

Proof drawings show what your child was thinking when solving the problem. It is important that children label their drawings to link them to the problem situation.

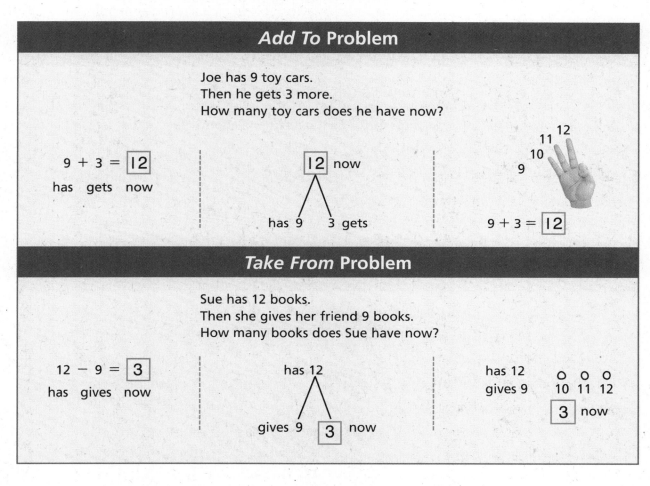

Add To Problem

Joe has 9 toy cars.
Then he gets 3 more.
How many toy cars does he have now?

$9 + 3 = \boxed{12}$

has gets now

$\boxed{12}$ now

has 9   3 gets

$9 + 3 = \boxed{12}$

Take From Problem

Sue has 12 books.
Then she gives her friend 9 books.
How many books does Sue have now?

$12 - 9 = \boxed{3}$

has gives now

has 12

gives 9 $\boxed{3}$ now

has 12
gives 9

o o o
10 11 12

$\boxed{3}$ now

Please call if you have any questions or concerns.

Sincerely,
Your child's teacher

CA CC

Unit 1 addresses the following standards from the *Common Core State Standards for Mathematics with California Additions*: **2.OA.1, 2.OA.2, 2.OA.3, 2.NBT.2, 2.NBT.5, 2.NBT.6, 2.NBT.9,** and all Mathematical Practices.

Estimada familia:

Su niño está aprendiendo a resolver problemas conocidos como problemas de *cambio al sumar* o de *cambio al restar*. Estos empiezan con una cantidad que luego es modificada por un cambio (algo que se suma o se resta), lo que resulta en una nueva cantidad.

Los dibujos muestran lo que su niño estaba pensando mientras resolvía el problema. Es importante que los niños rotulen sus dibujos para relacionarlos con la situación del problema.

Problema de *Cambio al sumar*

José tenía 9 carros de juguete.
Luego recibió 3 más.
¿Cuántos carros de juguete tiene ahora?

$9 + 3 = \boxed{12}$
tenía recibió ahora

$\boxed{12}$ ahora

tenía 9   3 recibió

$9 + 3 = \boxed{12}$

Problema de *Cambio al restar*

Susana tenía 12 libros.
Luego le dio 9 libros a su amigo.
¿Cuántos libros tiene ahora Susana?

$12 - 9 = \boxed{3}$
tenía dio ahora

tenía 12

dio 9 $\boxed{3}$ ahora

tenía 12
dio 9   o o o
          10 11 12

$\boxed{3}$ ahora

Si tiene alguna pregunta o algún comentario, por favor comuníquese conmigo.

Atentamente,
El maestro de su niño

CA CC

En la Unidad 1 se aplican los siguientes estándares auxiliares, contenidos en los *Estándares estatales comunes de matemáticas con adiciones para California*: **2.OA.1, 2.OA.2, 2.OA.3, 2.NBT.2, 2.NBT.5, 2.NBT.6, 2.NBT.9** y todos los de prácticas matemáticas.

Add To and *Take From* Word Problems

CA CC Content Standards **2.OA.1**
Mathematical Practices **MP.1, MP.2, MP.3, MP.4, MP.6**

Name _____

▶ Solve and Discuss

Make a drawing. Write an equation.
Solve the problem.

Show your work.

school

1. The school has 5 computers in
   the library. They buy some more
   computers. Now there are 12.
   How many computers does
   the school buy?

   ☐ _____
        label

beads

2. Alina has 17 beads. She uses 9 of
   them to make a bracelet. How many
   beads does she have left?

   ☐ _____
        label

party favors

3. Erin wraps 6 party favors. She needs
   to wrap 15 favors in all. How many
   favors does she still need to wrap?

   ☐ _____
        label

► **Solve and Discuss (continued)**

Make a drawing. Write an equation.
Solve the problem.

Show your work.

---

4. There are 16 children at the playground.
   Some children go home. Now there
   are 7 children at the playground.
   How many children went home?

children

   ☐ _____

   label

---

5. Lila has 6 stamps. Sam gives her
   some more stamps. Now Lila has
   14 stamps. How many stamps does
   Sam give Lila?

stamp

   ☐ _____

   label

---

6. There are 5 deer in the forest. 6 more
   deer enter the forest. How many deer
   are in the forest now?

forest

   ☐ _____

   label

Add To and *Take From* Word Problems

▶ Solve and Discuss

Make a drawing. Write an equation.
Solve the problem.

Show your work.

1. Moshe has 5 toy cars. Mary gives him
7 more toy cars. How many toy cars
does Moshe have now?

car

☐ _____
      label

2. Heather buys 5 puzzles at a yard sale.
Then her brother gives her some more.
Now she has a total of 11 puzzles.
How many puzzles did her brother
give her?

puzzle

☐ _____
      label

3. The cook has 16 bags of potatoes.
He uses some to make potato salad.
Now he has 7 bags of potatoes left.
How many bags did he use?

potatoes

☐ _____
      label

Name _____

▶ Solve and Discuss (continued)

Make a drawing. Write an equation.
Solve the problem.

Show your work.

4. Charisa buys 4 new books. Now she has 13 books. How many books did Charisa have before?

book

☐ _____
label

5. Shahla has 16 dolls. She gives 8 dolls to her sister. How many dolls does Shahla have now?

doll

☐ _____
label

6. Brian has some tomato plants in his garden. 9 of the plants are eaten by bugs. 4 plants are left. How many plants did Brian have in the beginning?

bug

☐ _____
label

Add To and *Take From* Problems—Unknown in All Positions

► **Solve and Discuss**

Make a drawing. Write an equation.
Solve the problem.

Show your work.

---

1. There are 13 people in a bike race. 8 are on top of the hill. The rest are at the bottom of the hill. How many people are at the bottom of the hill?

hill

☐ _____
      label

---

2. 4 horses are in the barn. 8 horses are in the field. How many horses are on the farm altogether?

horse

☐ _____
      label

---

3. Andrew makes some sandwiches. 6 are turkey sandwiches and 7 are ham sandwiches. How many sandwiches does Andrew make in all?

sandwich

☐ _____
      label

---

4. Keisha has 11 cousins. 4 are boys and the rest are girls. How many are girls?

girl

☐ _____
      label

▶ Solve and Discuss (continued)

Make a drawing. Write an equation.
Solve the problem.

Show your work.

---

5. Latisha has 16 bags. 8 are small and the rest are large. How many large bags does Latisha have?

bag

☐ _____
label

---

6. There are 7 books on the shelf and 5 on the table. How many books are there altogether?

book

☐ _____
label

---

7. Mandy sews 8 blue beads and 6 red beads on a ribbon. How many beads are on the ribbon?

ribbon

☐ _____
label

---

8. Lisa has 5 green pencils and some yellow pencils. She has 13 pencils in all. How many yellow pencils does Lisa have?

pencil

☐ _____
label

► Solve and Discuss

Make a drawing. Write an equation.
Solve the problem.

Show your work.

1. I have 12 flowers in a vase. 8 are daisies.
   The rest are roses. How many are roses?

   [ ] _____
         label

   rose

2. There are 13 animals at the animal shelter.
   7 of them are dogs. The rest are cats.
   How many cats are at the shelter?

   [ ] _____
         label

   animal
   shelter

3. Walt saw 4 crows. Then he saw some finches
   at the feeder. He saw 12 birds in all. How many
   finches were there?

   [ ] _____
         label

   finch

► You Decide

Complete this problem.

4. Jenna has 4 _____ and Bill

   has 6 _____. How many

   _____ do they have altogether?

   [ ] _____
         label

► Both Addends Unknown

5. Saira wants to put 7 flowers in a vase. She wants to use lilies and tulips. How many of each flower could she use?

☐ and ☐   7 = ☐ + ☐
lilies   tulips

☐ and ☐   7 = ☐ + ☐
lilies   tulips

☐ and ☐   7 = ☐ + ☐
lilies   tulips

☐ and ☐   7 = ☐ + ☐
lilies   tulips

☐ and ☐   7 = ☐ + ☐
lilies   tulips

☐ and ☐   7 = ☐ + ☐
lilies   tulips

Special *Put Together/ Take Apart* Problems

Name _____

CA CC Content Standards **2.OA.1, 2.OA.2**
Mathematical Practices **MP.1, MP.2**

VOCABULARY
more   fewer

▶ Solve and Discuss

Make a matching drawing or draw comparison bars.
Write an equation. Solve the problem.

Show your work.

---

1. Ben has 11 library books. If Ben returns 4 books,
   he will have as many library books as Dale. How
   many library books does Dale have?

library

☐ _____
        label

---

2. Shelley washes 14 cars. Amir washes 9 cars.
   How many **more** cars does Shelley wash
   than Amir?

car

☐ _____
        label

---

3. Gale has 6 peaches in a basket. If Gale gets
   5 more peaches, he will have as many peaches
   as Carl. How many peaches does Carl have?

basket

☐ _____
        label

---

4. Rob has 12 stamps. Ann has 5 **fewer** stamps.
   How many stamps does Ann have?

stamp

☐ _____
        label

▶ Solve and Discuss (continued)

Make a matching drawing or draw comparison bars.
Write an equation. Solve the problem.

---

5. Helena has 8 toys. If she gets 3 more, she will have as many toys as Matt. How many toys does Matt have?

toy

☐ _____
      label

---

6. Martin has 14 plants in his garden. Jacob has 5 fewer plants. How many plants does Jacob have?

garden

☐ _____
      label

---

7. Jana has 12 coins in her coin collection. Ari has 5 fewer coins. How many coins does Ari have?

coin

☐ _____
      label

▶ PATH to FLUENCY **Add and Subtract Within 20**

Add.

8. $5 + 6 = \boxed{}$ 9. $8 + 7 = \boxed{}$ 10. $13 + 0 = \boxed{}$

Subtract.

11. $14 - 6 = \boxed{}$ 12. $12 - 3 = \boxed{}$ 13. $11 - 9 = \boxed{}$

Compare Word Problems

▶ Solve and Discuss

Make a drawing. Write an equation.
Solve the problem.

Show your work.

1. Haley has 13 books in her bag. Gabrielle
   has 8 books in her bag. How many fewer
   books does Gabrielle have in her bag
   than Haley?

book

☐ _____
    label

2. Hannah has 11 stickers. Nat has 3 stickers.
   How many fewer stickers does Nat have
   than Hannah?

sticker

☐ _____
    label

3. An eraser costs 7 cents. A pencil costs
   9 cents more than an eraser. How many
   cents does a pencil cost?

pencil

☐ _____
    label

4. Linda has 11 cherries. If she eats 4 cherries,
   she will have the same number as Sally.
   How many cherries does Sally have?

cherries

☐ _____
    label

▶ Solve and Discuss (continued)

Make a drawing. Write an equation.
Solve the problem.

Show your work.

5. John has 8 notebooks. He has to get 6 more
   notebooks to have as many as Ben.
   How many notebooks does Ben have?

notebook

☐ _____
   label

6. Rasha solves 3 more puzzles than Leena.
   Leena solves 9 puzzles. How many
   puzzles does Rasha solve?

puzzle

☐ _____
   label

▶ What's the Error?

Latoya has 12 buttons. If she gives away 5 buttons,
she will have as many as Ron. How many buttons
does Ron have?

Did I make
a mistake?

7. Draw comparison bars to help Puzzled Penguin.

More Compare Word Problems

▶ Solve and Discuss

Make a drawing. Write an equation.
Solve the problem.

Show your work.

---

1. Erica has 13 color pencils. She has 8 at home and some at school. How many are at school?

school

☐ _____
  label

---

2. Joan has 15 toy guitars. Delia has 7 toy guitars. How many fewer toy guitars does Delia have than Joan?

guitar

☐ _____
  label

---

3. Ed has 14 puppets. He gives some to his brother. Now Ed has 5 puppets left. How many puppets does Ed give to his brother?

puppet

☐ _____
  label

---

4. Yolanda has a box of tennis balls. Alvin takes 7 of them. Now Yolanda has 5 left. How many tennis balls does Yolanda have in the beginning?

box

☐ _____
  label

► Solve and Discuss (continued)

Make a drawing. Write an equation.
Solve the problem.

Show your work.

5. Meena has 6 cherries. Anika gives
   her some more cherries. Meena has
   13 cherries now. How many cherries
   does Anika give Meena?

   ┌─────┐
   │   │ _____
   └─────┘
        label

cherry

6. Shane has 16 stamps. Dan has
   7 fewer stamps than Shane. How
   many stamps does Dan have?

   ┌─────┐
   │   │ _____
   └─────┘
        label

stamp

7. Lisha wants to put 15 apples in a bowl.
   She wants to use both green apples
   and red apples. How many of each could
   she use? Show three answers.

bowl

   ┌─────┐   ┌─────┐
   │   │ green apples and   │   │ red apples
   └─────┘   └─────┘

   ┌─────┐   ┌─────┐
   │   │ green apples and   │   │ red apples
   └─────┘   └─────┘

   ┌─────┐   ┌─────┐
   │   │ green apples and   │   │ red apples
   └─────┘   └─────┘

Mixed Word Problems

$5 + 7 = \boxed{}$

$6 + 7 = \boxed{}$

$9 + 9 = \boxed{}$

$8 + 7 = \boxed{}$

$9 + 7 = \boxed{}$

$3 + 8 = \boxed{}$

$4 + 8 = \boxed{}$

$5 + 8 = \boxed{}$

$6 + 8 = \boxed{}$

$7 + 8 = \boxed{}$

$8 + 8 = \boxed{}$

$9 + 8 = \boxed{}$

$3 + 9 = \boxed{}$

$4 + 9 = \boxed{}$

$5 + 9 = \boxed{}$

9 + 9 = $\boxed{18}$

| 9 | • | ••••• ••••• |

9 + 1 + 8

6 + 7 = $\boxed{13}$

| 7 | ••• | ••• |

7 + 3 + 3

5 + 7 = $\boxed{12}$

| 7 | ••• | •• |

7 + 3 + 2

3 + 8 = $\boxed{11}$

| 8 | •• | • |

8 + 2 + 1

9 + 7 = $\boxed{16}$

| 9 | • | ••••• |

9 + 1 + 6

8 + 7 = $\boxed{15}$

| 8 | •• | ••••• |

8 + 2 + 5

6 + 8 = $\boxed{14}$

| 8 | •• | •••• |

8 + 2 + 4

5 + 8 = $\boxed{13}$

| 8 | •• | ••• |

8 + 2 + 3

4 + 8 = $\boxed{12}$

| 8 | •• | •• |

8 + 2 + 2

9 + 8 = $\boxed{17}$

| 9 | • | ••••• •• |

9 + 1 + 7

8 + 8 = $\boxed{16}$

| 8 | •• | ••••• • |

8 + 2 + 6

7 + 8 = $\boxed{15}$

| 8 | •• | ••••• |

8 + 2 + 5

5 + 9 = $\boxed{14}$

| 9 | • | •••• |

9 + 1 + 4

4 + 9 = $\boxed{13}$

| 9 | • | ••• |

9 + 1 + 3

3 + 9 = $\boxed{12}$

| 9 | • | •• |

9 + 1 + 2

Green Make-a-Ten Cards

$6 + 9 = \boxed{}$

$7 + 9 = \boxed{}$

$7 + 4 = \boxed{}$

$8 + 4 = \boxed{}$

$9 + 4 = \boxed{}$

$6 + 5 = \boxed{}$

$7 + 5 = \boxed{}$

$8 + 5 = \boxed{}$

$9 + 5 = \boxed{}$

$5 + 6 = \boxed{}$

$8 + 9 = \boxed{}$

$7 + 6 = \boxed{}$

$8 + 6 = \boxed{}$

$9 + 6 = \boxed{}$

$4 + 7 = \boxed{}$

$7 + 4 = \boxed{11}$

| 7 | ••• • |

7 + 3 + 1

$7 + 9 = \boxed{16}$

| 9 | • ••••• |

9 + 1 + 6

$6 + 9 = \boxed{15}$

| 9 | • ••••• |

9 + 1 + 5

$6 + 5 = \boxed{11}$

| 6 | •••• • |

6 + 4 + 1

$9 + 4 = \boxed{13}$

| 9 | • ••• |

9 + 1 + 3

$8 + 4 = \boxed{12}$

| 8 | •• •• |

8 + 2 + 2

$9 + 5 = \boxed{14}$

| 9 | • •••• |

9 + 1 + 4

$8 + 5 = \boxed{13}$

| 8 | •• ••• |

8 + 2 + 3

$7 + 5 = \boxed{12}$

| 7 | ••• •• |

7 + 3 + 2

$7 + 6 = \boxed{13}$

| 7 | ••• ••• |

7 + 3 + 3

$8 + 9 = \boxed{17}$

| 9 | • •••••• |

9 + 1 + 7

$5 + 6 = \boxed{11}$

| 6 | •••• • |

6 + 4 + 1

$4 + 7 = \boxed{11}$

| 7 | ••• • |

7 + 3 + 1

$9 + 6 = \boxed{15}$

| 9 | • ••••• |

9 + 1 + 5

$8 + 6 = \boxed{14}$

| 8 | •• •••• |

8 + 2 + 4

Green Make-a-Ten Cards

▶ Complete and Solve Word Problems

Add information so you can solve the problems.
Then solve the problem.

Show your work.

---

1. Shannon makes a pitcher of lemonade. She uses
   8 lemons. How many lemons does she have left?

pitcher

_____

[ ] _____
          label

---

2. Sam walks his dog in the morning and again in
   the afternoon. Altogether Sam and the dog walk
   15 blocks. How far do they walk in the morning?

dog

_____

[ ] _____
          label

---

3. Kari makes a bracelet with blue and purple beads.
   6 beads are blue. How many beads are purple?

beads

_____

[ ] _____
          label

VOCABULARY
extra information

▶ Solve Problems with Extra Information

Cross out the **extra information**. Solve.

Show your work.

4. The dentist has 8 red toothbrushes and 6 green ones. Then she buys 9 more red ones. How many red toothbrushes does she have now?

☐ _____
label

toothbrush

5. Rosa has 5 gold coins and 6 silver coins in her collection. Her brother gives her 7 more gold coins. How many gold coins does Rosa have in all?

☐ _____
label

coin

6. Pam has 7 long ribbons and 9 short ribbons. She gives away 5 short ones. How many short ribbons does Pam have now?

☐ _____
label

ribbon

7. Franny has 8 kittens and 2 dogs. 4 kittens are asleep. How many kittens are awake?

☐ _____
label

dog

Problems with Not Enough, Extra, or Hidden Information

► **Find Information in a Story**

The Zoo

Today my class went to the zoo. I saw 4 elephants and 5 tigers. The giraffes were tall. There were 8 monkeys playing. I counted 13 penguins. I had fun at the zoo.

By Robbie

Use the story to solve the problems.   **Show your work.**

monkey

8. How many more monkeys than tigers did Robbie see?

☐ _____
      label

elephant

9. How many more penguins than elephants did Robbie see?

☐ _____
      label

penguin

10. How many fewer tigers than penguins did Robbie see?

☐ _____
      label

Name _____

VOCABULARY
hidden information

► Practice Solving Word Problems

Cross out extra information or write missing or **hidden information**. Solve the problem.

Show your work.

11. Chris washes some cars at the car wash. His friend Kelly washes some cars at the car wash. They wash a total of 16 cars. How many cars did Kelly wash?

car wash

_____

☐ _____
　　label

12. Shanna puts 13 markers and 6 crayons in her book bag. When she gets to school, she gives 4 of the markers to her friend. How many markers does Shanna have left?

marker

_____

☐ _____
　　label

13. There are 9 children and a set of triplets in the library. How many children are in the library?

library

_____

☐ _____
　　label

Problems with Not Enough, Extra, or Hidden Information

Name _____

CA CC Content Standards **2.0A.1**
Mathematical Practices **MP.1, MP.3, MP.4, MP.6, MP.7**

▶ Solve and Discuss

Draw comparison bars. Write an equation.
Solve the problem.

Show your work.

---

1. Darnell has 6 pens. That is 5 fewer pens
   than Natasha. How many pens does
   Natasha have?

   ☐ _____
   label

pen

---

2. There are 8 tigers at the Smithfield Zoo.
   The zoo has 9 more lions than tigers.
   How many lions does the zoo have?

   ☐ _____
   label

tiger

---

3. Sherean saves $7 more in October than
   in September. She saves $15 in October.
   How many dollars does she save
   in September?

   ☐ _____
   label

dollar

---

4. Nayoki makes 8 fewer airplane models
   than Maria. If Nayoki makes 9 airplane
   models, how many does Maria make?

   ☐ _____
   label

airplane
model

► Solve and Discuss (continued)

Draw comparison bars. Write an equation.
Solve the problem.

Show your work.

---

5. Chris catches 15 fish. Sean catches
9 fewer fish than Chris. How many fish
does Sean catch?

fish

☐ _____
       label

---

6. There are 9 more apples in the basket
than bananas. There are 17 apples in
the basket. How many bananas are in the
basket?

basket

☐ _____
       label

---

7. Maya has 8 fewer pennies than nickels.
How many nickels does she have if she
has 7 pennies?

nickel

☐ _____
       label

---

8. There are 5 more horses in the barn
than the field. There are 12 horses in the
barn. How many horses are in the field?

barn

☐ _____
       label

More Complex *Compare* Problems

Name _____

CA CC Content Standards **2.0A.1, 2.0A.2**
Mathematical Practices **MP.1, MP.3, MP.4, MP.6, MP.7**

► Model Two-Step Word Problems

Solve the two-step word problem.   Show your work.

I. Lindsay brings in 5 cans for the school food drive. Olivia brings in 4 more cans than Lindsay. Matt brings in 6 more cans than Olivia. How many cans does Matt bring?

A. How many cans does Olivia bring?

[   ] _____
          label

B. How many cans does Matt bring?

[   ] _____
          label

▶ Model Two-Step Word Problems (continued)

Solve the two-step word problem.

Show your work.

2. There are 14 computers in the school library. 5 girls and 3 boys are each using a computer right now. How many more children can use a computer?

A. How many children are using computers right now?

☐ _____
   label

B. How many more children can use a computer?

☐ _____
   label

Two-Step Word Problems

▶ Solve Two-Step Word Problems

Think about the first-step question.
Then solve the problem.

Show your work.

3. Mari has 17 tomatoes. She uses 9 tomatoes to make a sauce. Then she makes a salad with 4 tomatoes. How many tomatoes does she have left?

tomato

☐ _____
label

4. There are 16 robins in a tree. 9 robins fly away. Then 4 blue jays fly into the tree. How many birds are in the tree now?

robin

☐ _____
label

5. Julie has 6 red pencils. She has 2 more blue pencils than red pencils. How many pencils does she have in all?

pencil

☐ _____
label

▶ Solve Two-Step Word Problems (continued)

Think about the first-step question.   Show your work.
Then solve the problem.

---

6. Lana had 9 sheep and some horses on her farm.
   Altogether there were 17 animals. Her grandmother
   gives her 3 more horses. How many horses does
   she have on the farm now?

sheep

   ☐ _____
        label

---

7. Rafa has 13 marbles. He has 6 red marbles and
   the rest are green. Mia gives him some more green
   marbles. Now Rafa has 12 green marbles. How
   many green marbles does Mia give Rafa?

marbles

   ☐ _____
        label

▶ PATH to FLUENCY Add and Subtract Within 20

Add.

8. $4 + 6 =$ ☐   9. $5 + 7 =$ ☐   10. $9 + 6 =$ ☐

Subtract.

11. $18 - 9 =$ ☐   12. $12 - 8 =$ ☐   13. $11 - 3 =$ ☐

Name _____

CA CC Content Standards **2.OA.1**
Mathematical Practices **MP.1, MP.3, MP.4, MP.6**

▶ Solve and Discuss

Make a drawing. Write an equation.
Solve the problem.   **Show your work.**

---

1. Mina buys some new shirts. She returns 4 shirts
   to the store. Now she has 8 new shirts. How many
   shirts does Mina buy at first?

   store

   ☐ _____
        label

---

2. Marie buys 8 peaches and a dozen apples.
   That is 6 fewer peaches than Rubin buys.
   How many peaches does Rubin buy?

   peach

   ☐ _____
        label

---

3. There are 17 children in the class play.
   9 are boys and the rest are girls.
   Then 3 more girls join the play. How many
   girls are in the play?

   children

   ☐ _____
        label

---

4. Ed buys 9 books at one store and 3 books at another.
   He buys 8 more books than Brenda. How many
   books does Brenda buy?

   book

   ☐ _____
        label

► **Solve and Discuss (continued)**

Make a drawing. Write an equation.
Solve the problem.   Show your work.

---

5. There are some cows in a field. 4 horses join them.
   Now there are 12 animals in the field. How many
   cows are in the field?

   horse

   ☐ _____
          label

---

6. Rob sells 6 skateboards on Friday, 3 skateboards on
   Saturday, and 2 skateboards on Sunday. How many
   skateboards does he sell altogether?

   skateboard

   ☐ _____
          label

► **What's the Error?**

Felix has 7 white potatoes, 8 purple potatoes,
and 5 green apples. He uses all the potatoes to
make a soup. How many potatoes does Felix use?

$$7 + 8 + 5 = 20 \text{ potatoes}$$
$$\text{w} \quad \text{p} \quad \text{g}$$

Did I make a mistake?

7. Help Puzzled Penguin.

$15 - 6 = \boxed{}$ $16 - 7 = \boxed{}$ $11 - 7 = \boxed{}$

$12 - 8 = \boxed{}$ $13 - 9 = \boxed{}$ $11 - 6 = \boxed{}$

$12 - 7 = \boxed{}$ $13 - 8 = \boxed{}$ $14 - 9 = \boxed{}$

$11 - 5 = \boxed{}$ $17 - 8 = \boxed{}$ $13 - 7 = \boxed{}$

$14 - 8 = \boxed{}$ $15 - 9 = \boxed{}$ $11 - 4 = \boxed{}$

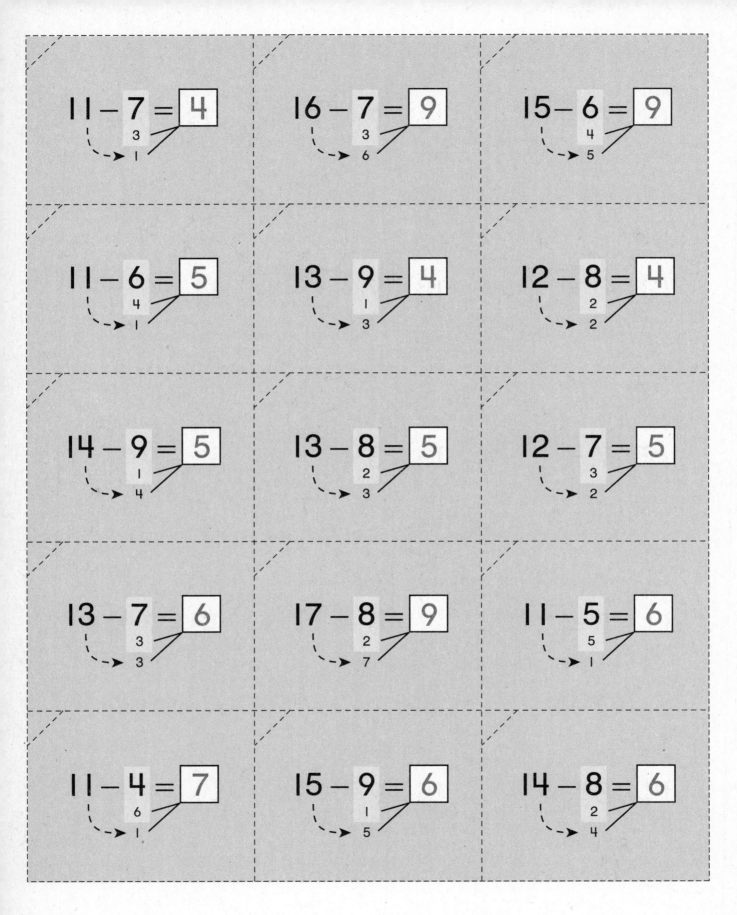

11 − 7 = 4
3
1

16 − 7 = 9
3
6

15 − 6 = 9
4
5

11 − 6 = 5
4
1

13 − 9 = 4
1
3

12 − 8 = 4
2
2

14 − 9 = 5
1
4

13 − 8 = 5
2
3

12 − 7 = 5
3
2

13 − 7 = 6
3
3

17 − 8 = 9
2
7

11 − 5 = 6
5
1

11 − 4 = 7
6
1

15 − 9 = 6
1
5

14 − 8 = 6
2
4

Blue Make-a-Ten Cards

12 − 5 = ☐

13 − 6 = ☐

18 − 9 = ☐

15 − 8 = ☐

16 − 9 = ☐

11 − 3 = ☐

12 − 4 = ☐

13 − 5 = ☐

14 − 6 = ☐

15 − 7 = ☐

16 − 8 = ☐

17 − 9 = ☐

12 − 3 = ☐

13 − 4 = ☐

14 − 5 = ☐

$$18 - 9 = \boxed{9}$$
$$\begin{array}{c} 1 \\ 8 \end{array}$$

$$13 - 6 = \boxed{7}$$
$$\begin{array}{c} 4 \\ 3 \end{array}$$

$$12 - 5 = \boxed{7}$$
$$\begin{array}{c} 5 \\ 2 \end{array}$$

$$11 - 3 = \boxed{8}$$
$$\begin{array}{c} 7 \\ 1 \end{array}$$

$$16 - 9 = \boxed{7}$$
$$\begin{array}{c} 1 \\ 6 \end{array}$$

$$15 - 8 = \boxed{7}$$
$$\begin{array}{c} 2 \\ 5 \end{array}$$

$$14 - 6 = \boxed{8}$$
$$\begin{array}{c} 4 \\ 4 \end{array}$$

$$13 - 5 = \boxed{8}$$
$$\begin{array}{c} 5 \\ 3 \end{array}$$

$$12 - 4 = \boxed{8}$$
$$\begin{array}{c} 6 \\ 2 \end{array}$$

$$17 - 9 = \boxed{8}$$
$$\begin{array}{c} 1 \\ 7 \end{array}$$

$$16 - 8 = \boxed{8}$$
$$\begin{array}{c} 2 \\ 6 \end{array}$$

$$15 - 7 = \boxed{8}$$
$$\begin{array}{c} 3 \\ 5 \end{array}$$

$$14 - 5 = \boxed{9}$$
$$\begin{array}{c} 5 \\ 4 \end{array}$$

$$13 - 4 = \boxed{9}$$
$$\begin{array}{c} 6 \\ 3 \end{array}$$

$$12 - 3 = \boxed{9}$$
$$\begin{array}{c} 7 \\ 2 \end{array}$$

Blue Make-a-Ten Cards

► Math and Healthy Food

Beren and her friends are making funny face pizzas.

1. Darryl uses 2 green olives for eyes and 9 black olives to make a big smile. How many olives does he use?

   [ ] _____
         label

2. Sarah uses 6 fewer mushroom slices than Darryl. Sarah uses 8 slices. How many slices does Darryl use?

   [ ] _____
         label

3. When they start making the pizzas, there are a dozen small tomatoes. Darryl uses 2 tomatoes. Beren and Dawn each use 1 tomato. No one else uses any. How many tomatoes are left?

   [ ] _____
         label

Name _____

► **Problems with Extra Information**

Solve. Cross out the information you do not need.   **Show your work.**

4. Beren makes a fruit salad. She uses 2 strawberries,
   8 blueberries, 7 raspberries, and 3 apples.
   How many berries does she use?

   ☐ _____
   label

5. Darryl makes a snack mix. He uses 2 cups of cereal,
   4 cups of raisins, 3 cups of dried cherries, and
   2 cups of walnuts. How many more cups of dried fruit
   does he use than cups of nuts?

   ☐ _____
   label

► **Write and Solve a Problem**

"Ants on a Log" is a snack made with celery, peanut butter,
and raisins.

Beren's Snack	**Darryl's Snack**	**Sarah's Snack**

6. Use the pictures. On a separate sheet of paper, write
   a problem.

   Exchange with a classmate. Solve each other's problem.

Focus on Mathematical Practices

Write each addition or subtraction in the box below
the correct answer.

1. $0 + 7$ $7 + 7$ $12 - 5$ $20 - 6$ $13 - 1$

7	12	14

Write the partner or total in the box.

2. $5 + 0 = \boxed{}$

3. $15 - 6 = \boxed{}$

4. $\boxed{} = 3 + 8$

5. $3 + 4 + 6 = \boxed{}$

6. $7 + 9 = \boxed{}$

7. $15 - 8 = \boxed{}$

Is the total 12? Choose Yes or No.

8. $5 + 6$ ○ Yes   ○ No

$7 + 5$ ○ Yes   ○ No

$12 + 0$ ○ Yes   ○ No

$4 + 9$ ○ Yes   ○ No

$2 + 10$ ○ Yes   ○ No

9. Complete the Math Mountain.

   Write an addition and a subtraction
   equation to go with it.

   _____

   _____

   How are the equations related?

   _____

   _____

_____

Solve.

10. Beth has a bag of apples. She gives 3 apples to
    Natasha. Now she has 15 apples left. How many
    apples were in the bag at first?

    ☐ _____
        label

_____

11. Evan finds 12 shells. Aaron finds 5 fewer shells
    than Evan. How many shells does Aaron find?

    ☐ _____
        label

12. Make a drawing. Write an equation.
Solve the problem.

Linda sees 18 cows and 12 horses in a field.
Eight of the cows are brown. The rest are white.
How many cows are white?

```
┌──────────────────────────────────────────┐
│                                            │
│   ┌────┐                                   │
│   │    │   _____                │
│   └────┘         label                     │
│                                            │
│                                            │
└──────────────────────────────────────────┘
```

13. Choose an even number. Write a doubles addition
equation with your number. Explain how you know
the total is even.

_____

_____

Match each addition or subtraction to the correct answer.

14. 2 + 4 + 6 •   • 9

   16 − 8 •   • 12

   13 + 7 •   • 20

   14 − 5 •   • 8

Solve. Circle the correct answer.

15. There are some frogs on a rock. Nine more frogs jump on the rock. Now there are 14 frogs. How many frogs were on the rock at first?

There were
| 5 |
| 6 |
| 13 |
frogs on the rock at first.

16. There are 6 basketballs, 3 footballs, and 9 baseballs on the playground. How many balls are on the playground?

There are
| 16 |
| 18 |
| 19 |
balls on the playground.

17. Draw comparison bars. Write an equation. Solve the problem.

Madison has 11 grapes in a bowl. Hailey has 5 more grapes than Madison. How many grapes does Hailey have?

_____
label

Dear Family:

Your child is learning about place value and will use this knowledge to add 2- and 3-digit numbers.

As we begin this unit, your child will represent numbers using drawings like this one:

Then, children will begin to represent numbers using Quick Hundreds and Quick Tens.

Quick Hundred   Quick Tens   Ones

Name a 2- or 3-digit number and ask your child to make a drawing to represent that number.

Later in this unit, children will work on adding 2-digit numbers using the drawings to help them.

Thank you. Please call or write if you have any questions.

Sincerely,
Your child's teacher

CA CC

Unit 2 addresses the following standards from the *Common Core State Standards for Mathematics with California Additions*: **2.OA.1, 2.OA.2, 2.NBT.1, 2.NBT.1a, 2.NBT.2, 2.NBT.3, 2.NBT.4, 2.NBT.5, 2.NBT.6, 2.NBT.7, 2.NBT.8, 2.NBT.9, 2.MD.8**, and all Mathematical Practices.

Estimada familia:

Su niño está aprendiendo acerca del valor posicional y usará esos conocimientos para sumar números de 2 y 3 dígitos.

Cuando comencemos con esta unidad, su niño representará números usando dibujos como este:

Luego, los niños comenzarán a representar números usando "Centenas rápidas" y "Decenas rápidas".

Centena rápida   Decenas rápidas   Unidades

146

100   +   40   +   6

Diga un número de 2 ó 3 dígitos y pida a su niño que haga un dibujo para representar ese número.

Más adelante, los niños trabajarán sumando números de 2 dígitos y usarán los dibujos como ayuda.

Gracias. Si tiene alguna pregunta, por favor comuníquese conmigo.

Atentamente,
El maestro de su niño

 CA CC

En la Unidad 2 se aplican los siguientes estándares auxiliares, contenidos en los *Estándares estatales comunes de matemáticas con adiciones para California*: **2.OA.1, 2.OA.2, 2.NBT.1, 2.NBT.1a, 2.NBT.2, 2.NBT.3, 2.NBT.4, 2.NBT.5, 2.NBT.6, 2.NBT.7, 2.NBT.8, 2.NBT.9, 2.MD.8** y todos los de prácticas matemáticas.

►Write the Numbers 101 to 200

I. Write the numbers going down to see the tens.

101	111							
102		122		152				
103					163			193
			144					
						185		
	116			156				
		128						
							189	
110	120			150		170		200

► Word Problem Practice: Addition and Subtraction Within 20

Solve.

Show your work.

2. Sara has some marbles. Shane gives her 8 more marbles. Now Sara has 17 marbles. How many marbles did Sara have at first?

marbles

☐ _____
label

3. There are 14 children on the soccer field. There are 8 boys and the rest are girls. Then 2 girls leave the soccer field. How many girls are on the soccer field now?

soccer field

☐ _____
label

4. Tom has 6 fewer pencils than Ari. Tom has 7 pencils. How many pencils does Ari have?

pencil

☐ _____
label

5. In the lunchroom, 16 children have apples. Nine of these children have red apples and the rest have green apples. Then 5 more children come with green apples. How many children have green apples now?

apple

☐ _____
label

1	2	10	20
1	2	1 0	2 0

3	4	30	40
3	4	3 0	4 0

5	6	50	60
5	6	5 0	6 0

7	8	70	80
7	8	7 0	8 0

9	90	100
9	9 0	1 0 0

Secret Code Cards (1–100)

► Add Tens or Ones

Add.

1. $10 + 20 =$ _____ $70 + 20 =$ _____ $60 + 30 =$ _____

    $1 + 2 =$ _____ $7 + 2 =$ _____ $6 + 3 =$ _____

2. $20 + 70 =$ _____ $30 + 50 =$ _____ $40 + 50 =$ _____

    $2 + 7 =$ _____ $3 + 5 =$ _____ $4 + 5 =$ _____

3. $30 + 60 =$ _____ $20 + 80 =$ _____ $50 + 40 =$ _____

    $3 + 6 =$ _____ $2 + 8 =$ _____ $5 + 4 =$ _____

4. $50 + 50 =$ _____ $80 + 20 =$ _____ $40 + 60 =$ _____

    $5 + 5 =$ _____ $8 + 2 =$ _____ $4 + 6 =$ _____

5. $90 + 10 =$ _____ $90 + 20 =$ _____ $40 + 30 =$ _____

    $9 + 1 =$ _____ $9 + 2 =$ _____ $4 + 3 =$ _____

6. $50 + 20 =$ _____ $20 + 30 =$ _____ $60 + 70 =$ _____

    $5 + 2 =$ _____ $2 + 3 =$ _____ $6 + 7 =$ _____

Name _____

▶ Word Problem Practice: Addition and Subtraction Within 20

Solve.

7. There are 18 children in the library. 9 children leave the library. Then 3 more children come. How many children are in the library now?

library

☐ _____
    label

8. Some crayons are on the table. Mrs. Spain takes 5 of the crayons. Now there are 8 crayons on the table. How many crayons were on the table before?

crayon

☐ _____
    label

9. The jewelry store has 8 red bracelets and some blue bracelets. There are 15 bracelets in all. Then 3 blue bracelets are sold. How many blue bracelets are still in the store?

bracelet

☐ _____
    label

10. Mr. Rivera bakes 7 banana muffins and 9 orange muffins. He gives some muffins to his friends. Now he has 8 muffins. How many muffins does he give to his friends?

muffin

☐ _____
    label

Draw Quick Tens and Quick Hundreds

Name

CA CC Content Standards **2.NBT.1, 2.NBT.2, 2.NBT.3**
Mathematical Practices **MP.2, MP.7**

VOCABULARY
expanded form

► Hundreds, Tens, and Ones

Draw the number using hundred boxes, ten sticks, and circles. Then write the **expanded form**.

1. 106	2. 122	3. 139
$\underline{100} + \underline{0} + \underline{6}$	___ + ___ + ___	___ + ___ + ___

What number is shown?   H = Hundreds, T = Tens, O = Ones

4.

$\underline{1}$ H $\underline{4}$ T $\underline{7}$ O

$\underline{147} = \underline{100} + \underline{40} + \underline{7}$

5.

___ H ___ T ___ O

___ = ___ + ___ + ___

6.

___ H ___ T ___ O

___ = ___ + ___ + ___

7.

___ H ___ T ___ O

___ = ___ + ___ + ___

VOCABULARY
number name

▶ **Read and Write Number Names**

1 one	11 eleven	10 ten	100 one hundred
2 two	12 twelve	20 twenty	
3 three	13 thirteen	30 thirty	
4 four	14 fourteen	40 forty	
5 five	15 fifteen	50 fifty	
6 six	16 sixteen	60 sixty	
7 seven	17 seventeen	70 seventy	
8 eight	18 eighteen	80 eighty	
9 nine	19 nineteen	90 ninety	

Write the number.

8. thirty-five _____   **9.** seventy-two _____

10. fifty-four _____   **11.** eighty-nine _____

12. sixty-three _____   **13.** ninety-one _____

Write the **number name**.

14. 47 _____   **15.** 62 _____

16. 85 _____   **17.** 94 _____

18. 28 _____   **19.** 86 _____

Represent Write the number name, then
draw Quick Tens and ones in the box.

20. 60 _____

21. 72 _____

Represent Numbers in Different Ways

2-4
Class Activity

Name _____

CA CC Content Standards **2.NBT.1, 2.NBT.1a, 2.NBT.3, 2.NBT.5, 2.NBT.7, 2.NBT.8**
Mathematical Practices **MP.1, MP.2, MP.4, MP.7**

► Word Problems with Groups of Ten

Solve. Make a proof drawing.   **Show your work.**

1. Remah has 34 stickers. Only 10 stickers fit on a page in her scrapbook. How many pages can she fill with stickers? How many stickers will be left over?

   ☐ pages   ☐ stickers left over

2. David has 42 beads. He wants to make some necklaces that use 10 beads each. How many necklaces can he make? How many beads will be left over?

   ☐ necklaces   ☐ beads left over

3. The team wants to buy T-shirts that cost 10 dollars each. They have 57 dollars. How many T-shirts can they buy? How many dollars will be left over?

   ☐ T-shirts   ☐ dollars left over

4. The store has 163 apples. Each basket can hold 10 apples. How many baskets can they fill with apples? How many apples will be left over?

   ☐ baskets   ☐ apples left over

▶ Add 1, 10, or 100

Add.

5. $38 + 1 =$ _____

6. $9 + 10 =$ _____

7. $24 + 100 =$ _____

8. $150 + 1 =$ _____

9. $7 + 100 =$ _____

10. $92 + 10 =$ _____

11. $59 + 1 =$ _____

12. $166 + 10 =$ _____

13. $10 + 10 =$ _____

14. $143 + 1 =$ _____

15. $98 + 100 =$ _____

16. $46 + 10 =$ _____

17. $11 + 100 =$ _____

18. $195 + 1 =$ _____

19. $104 + 10 =$ _____

20. $30 + 100 =$ _____

CA CC Content Standards **2.NBT.1, 2.NBT.3, 2.NBT.4**
Mathematical Practices **MP.2, MP.3, MP.6, MP.8**

Name

▶Use Drawings to Compare Numbers

Use these symbols to compare numbers.

< **is less than**   > **is greater than**   = **is equal to**

Make a drawing for each number. Write <, >, or =.

1.   56 ◯ 81   2.   123 ◯ 109

3.   101 ◯ 101   4.   98 ◯ 150

5.   67 ◯ 76   6.   120 ◯ 102

Name _____

► **Compare Numbers**

Write <, >, or =.

7. 135 ◯ 137

8. 83 ◯ 83

9. 119 ◯ 87

10. 127 ◯ 172

11. 62 ◯ 57

12. 51 ◯ 15

13. 111 ◯ 111

14. 37 ◯ 74

15. 192 ◯ 191

16. 100 ◯ 10

► **What's the Error?**

149 (>) 176

I know that 9 is greater than 6. Did I make a mistake?

17. Draw a proof drawing to help Puzzled Penguin.
   Write <, >, or =.

149 ◯ 176

Content Overview

Dear Family:

Your child is now learning how to add 2-digit numbers. The "big mystery" in adding is making a new ten or a new hundred. Children can write this new group in several ways.

Show All Totals	New Groups Below
45 + 28 Add tens. → 60 Add ones. → 13 ——— 73 Find total tens. Find total ones.	45 + 28 ——— 73 New ten

Show All Totals — New ten

New Groups Below:

Find total ones. (13) Write 3 and put the new ten in the tens column ready to add.

Add the tens. (4 + 2 = 6, 6 + 1 = 7)

New Groups Above

1
45
+ 28
———
73

Children usually find it easier to write the new ten below because then they add the new ten last. They add 4 + 2 = 6 and then 6 + 1 = 7.

Traditionally, most children have learned to write the new ten above. With this method, you add 1 + 4 = 5 and then 5 + 2 = 7. This is more difficult for many children, but some children may still choose this method, particularly if they have been taught to do so previously.

Thank you for helping your child learn mathematics.

Sincerely,
Your child's teacher

© Houghton Mifflin Harcourt Publishing Company

 CA CC

Unit 2 addresses the following standards from the *Common Core State Standards for Mathematics with California Additions*: **2.OA.1, 2.OA.2, 2.NBT.1, 2.NBT.1a, 2.NBT.2, 2.NBT.3, 2.NBT.4, 2.NBT.5, 2.NBT.6, 2.NBT.7, 2.NBT.8, 2.NBT.9, 2.MD.8,** and all Mathematical Practices.

Carta a la familia

Un vistazo general al contenido

Estimada familia:

Su niño está aprendiendo a sumar números de 2 dígitos. El "gran misterio" en la suma de números de 2 dígitos consiste en formar una nueva decena o una nueva centena. Los niños pueden anotar este nuevo grupo de varias maneras.

Mostrar todos los totales	Grupos nuevos abajo
$\begin{array}{r} 45 \\ + 28 \\ \hline \end{array}$ Sumar decenas. → 60 Sumar unidades. → 13 73 Hallar el total de decenas. Hallar el total de unidades. Nueva decena	$\begin{array}{r} 45 \\ + 28 \\ \hline 73 \end{array}$ Nueva decena Hallar el total de unidades. (13) Escribir 3 y poner la nueva decena en la columna de las decenas, lista para sumar. Sumar las decenas. (4 + 2 = 6, 6 + 1 = 7)

Grupos nuevos arriba

$\begin{array}{r} 1 \\ 45 \\ + 28 \\ \hline 73 \end{array}$

Por lo general a los niños les resulta más fácil escribir la nueva decena abajo, porque entonces suman la nueva decena al final. Suman 4 + 2 = 6 y luego 6 + 1 = 7.

Tradicionalmente, la mayoría de los estudiantes han aprendido a escribir la nueva decena arriba. Con ese método, se suma 1 + 4 = 5 y luego 5 + 2 = 7. Para muchos niños ese método resulta más difícil pero algunos siguen escogiéndolo, en especial si ya lo han aprendido.

Gracias por ayudar a su niño a aprender matemáticas.

Atentamente,
El maestro de su niño

CA CC

En la Unidad 2 se aplican los siguientes estándares auxiliares, contenidos en los *Estándares estatales comunes de matemáticas con adiciones para California*: **2.OA.1, 2.OA.2, 2.NBT.1, 2.NBT.1a, 2.NBT.2, 2.NBT.3, 2.NBT.4, 2.NBT.5, 2.NBT.6, 2.NBT.7, 2.NBT.8, 2.NBT.9, 2.MD.8** y todos los de prácticas matemáticas.

Explore 2-Digit Addition

2-6
Class Activity

CA CC Content Standards 2.OA.2, 2.NBT.1, 2.NBT.1a, 2.NBT.6, 2.NBT.9
Mathematical Practices MP.1, MP.3, MP.4, MP.6, MP.7

Name _____

▶ The New Ten

Solve each word problem.

Show your work.

1. Mr. Green puts 56 red peppers in the vegetable bin. Mrs. Green puts 28 yellow peppers in the bin. How many peppers do they put in the bin altogether?

   ☐☐☐ _____
   label

2. Mrs. Green stacks 43 tomatoes. Mr. Green adds 39 more. How many tomatoes do they stack in all?

   ☐☐☐ _____
   label

▶ The New Hundred

3. Mr. Green counts 65 cans. Mrs. Green counts 82 cans. How many cans do they count in all?

   ☐☐☐ _____
   label

4. Mrs. Green counts 57 bags of beans. Mr. Green counts 71 bags of beans. How many bags of beans do they count in all?

   ☐☐☐ _____
   label

▶ Make a Ten or Hundred

Solve each word problem.

Show your work.

5. Mrs. Green stacks 37 boxes of mushrooms.
   Mr. Green stacks 29 boxes of mushrooms.
   How many boxes do they stack altogether?

   ☐ _____
   label

6. Mr. Green sells 65 bananas.
   Mrs. Green sells 54 bananas.
   How many bananas do they sell in all?

   ☐ _____
   label

▶ PATH to FLUENCY Add and Subtract Within 20

Add.

7. $6 + 8 =$ _____

8. $9 + 7 =$ _____

9. $6 + 10 =$ _____

10. $\begin{array}{r} 9 \\ +\ 4 \\ \hline \end{array}$

11. $\begin{array}{r} 10 \\ +\ 1 \\ \hline \end{array}$

12. $\begin{array}{r} 7 \\ +\ 6 \\ \hline \end{array}$

Subtract.

13. $15 - 7 =$ _____

14. $20 - 10 =$ _____

15. $18 - 9 =$ _____

16. $\begin{array}{r} 11 \\ -\ 6 \\ \hline \end{array}$

17. $\begin{array}{r} 15 \\ -\ 8 \\ \hline \end{array}$

18. $\begin{array}{r} 16 \\ -\ 7 \\ \hline \end{array}$

Name _____

CA CC Content Standards **2.OA.1, 2.NBT.1, 2.NBT.1a, 2.NBT.7, 2.NBT.9**
Mathematical Practices **MP.1, MP.2, MP.4**

▶ Show All Totals Method

Solve. Make a proof drawing.   Show your work.

1. Mr. Green orders 25 jars of grape jelly
   and 48 jars of strawberry jelly. How many
   jars of jelly does he order?

   ☐☐☐ _____
        label

2. Mrs. Green orders 65 pounds of bananas.
   That is not enough, so she orders
   29 more pounds. How many pounds does
   she order altogether?

   ☐☐☐ _____
        label

3. Mrs. Green orders 78 pounds of white
   rice and 57 pounds of brown rice. How
   many pounds of rice does she order?

   ☐☐☐ _____
        label

4. Mr. Green orders 49 jars of plain
   peanut butter and 86 jars of chunky
   peanut butter. How many jars of peanut
   butter does he order in all?

   ☐☐☐ _____
        label

▶ Word Problem Practice: Two-Step Problems

Solve.

5. There were 17 plums on the table. Nine plums were sold. Mr. Green puts some more plums on the table. Now there are 13 plums. How many plums did Mr. Green put on the table?

plum

☐ _____
       label

6. Some carrots are in a basket. Fran adds 5 more carrots to the basket. James places 4 more carrots there. Now there are 13 carrots. How many carrots were in the basket in the beginning?

carrots

☐ _____
       label

7. Jane buys 8 bananas. Damon buys 4 fewer bananas than Jane. How many bananas do they buy in all?

bananas

☐ _____
       label

8. There were 7 bags of green grapes and some bags of red grapes. There were 15 bags of grapes in all. Then 3 bags of red grapes were sold. How many bags of red grapes are left?

grapes

☐ _____
       label

Addition–Show All Totals Method

Name

CA CC Content Standards **2.NBT.1, 2.NBT.1a, 2.NBT.6, 2.NBT.7, 2.NBT.9**
Mathematical Practices **MP.1, MP.2, MP.3, MP.6**

► **Practice and Share**

Add. Use any method.

$$
\begin{array}{r} 86 \\ +\ 57 \\ \hline 130 \\ +\ 13 \\ \hline 143 \end{array}
\qquad \text{or} \qquad
\begin{array}{r} 86 \\ +\ 57 \\ \hline +++ \\ 143 \end{array}
$$

$$130 + 13 = 143$$

1.
$$
\begin{array}{r} 39 \\ +97 \\ \hline \end{array}
\qquad\qquad
\begin{array}{r} 83 \\ +39 \\ \hline \end{array}
$$

2.
$$
\begin{array}{r} 58 \\ +87 \\ \hline \end{array}
\qquad\qquad
\begin{array}{r} 72 \\ +37 \\ \hline \end{array}
$$

3.
$$
\begin{array}{r} 49 \\ +85 \\ \hline \end{array}
\qquad\qquad
\begin{array}{r} 94 \\ +52 \\ \hline \end{array}
$$

▶ Predict New Ten or New Hundred

Add. Use any method.

4. $\begin{array}{r} 61 \\ +37 \\ \hline \end{array}$ $\begin{array}{r} 53 \\ +98 \\ \hline \end{array}$

5. $\begin{array}{r} 42 \\ +80 \\ \hline \end{array}$ $\begin{array}{r} 66 \\ +27 \\ \hline \end{array}$

▶ What's the Error?

$\begin{array}{r} 38 \\ +46 \\ \hline 74 \end{array}$

I know that 3 tens plus 4 tens equals 7 tens. Did I make a mistake?

6. Show Puzzled Penguin how you would add the numbers.
   Draw a proof diagram to check your work.

$\begin{array}{r} 38 \\ +46 \\ \hline \end{array}$

▶ What's the Error?

```
   32
 + 25
 ─────
   67
```

Did I make a mistake?

1. Add. Make a proof drawing.

```
   32
 + 25
 ─────
```

```
   48
 + 43
 ─────
  8 11
```

Is this correct?

2. Add. Make a proof drawing.

```
   48
 + 43
 ─────
```

► What's the Error? (continued)

$$\overset{1}{17}$$
$$+\ 66$$
$$\overline{74}$$

Is this one correct?

3. Add. Make a proof drawing.

$$17$$
$$+\ 66$$

$$\overset{3}{39}$$
$$+\ 54$$
$$\overline{111}$$

Did I add correctly this time?

4. Add. Make a proof drawing.

$$39$$
$$+\ 54$$

► Choose a Method

Add. Use any method.

5.

73	26	58
+ 42	+ 85	+ 34

Choose an Addition Method

Cut along the dashed lines.

Dollar Bills

► Find the Amount

Write the answer using ¢.
Then write the answer using $.

Show your work.

1. Joe has 11 dimes and 4 pennies. How much money does Joe have?

_____   _____

2. Bekah has one dollar, 3 dimes, and 8 pennies. How much money does Bekah have?

_____   _____

3. Tim has 14 dimes and 15 pennies. How much money does Tim have?

_____   _____

4. Dinah has 2 dimes, 6 pennies, and 1 dollar. How much money does Dinah have?

_____   _____

5. Lou has 1 dollar, 8 dimes, and 19 pennies. How much money does Lou have?

_____   _____

Name _____

▶ The Farm Stand

Potatoes 65¢	**Corn** 56¢	**Bananas** 89¢	**Peaches** 77¢
Radishes 76¢	**Lemons** 88¢	**Celery** 57¢	**Peppers** 78¢
Mushrooms 67¢	**Carrots** 86¢	**Tomatoes** 97¢	**Grapes** 98¢
Watermelon 59¢	**Oranges** 85¢	**Raspberries** 99¢	**Green Beans** 87¢

Buy with Pennies and Dimes

Name

CA CC Content Standards **2.NBT.2, 2.MD.8**
Mathematical Practices **MP.2, MP.4, MP.7**

► **Practice Counting by 5s**

1. Go across. Loop groups of 5 bags. Write the numbers.

1 2 3 4   6 7 8 9

11 12 13 14   16 17 18 19

21 22 23 24   26 27 28 29

31 32 33 34   36 37 38 39

41 42 43 44   46 47 48 49

51 52 53 54   56 57 58 59

61 62 63 64   66 67 68 69

71 72 73 74   76 77 78 79

81 82 83 84   86 87 88 89

91 92 93 94   96 97 98 99

► How Many Cents?

Under the coins, write the total amount of money so far.
Then write the total using $. The first one is done for you.

2.   5¢   5¢   5¢

 5¢   10¢   15¢ $ _0_ . _1_ _5_
                                    total

---

3.   5¢   5¢   5¢   5¢

____   ____   ____   ____ $ __ . __ __
                                    total

---

4.   5¢   5¢   5¢   5¢   5¢

____ ____ ____ ____ ____ $ __ . __ __
                                    total

---

5. Pedro has 9 nickels. Draw ⑤s.

Write the total amount of money. $ __ . __ __
                                            total

Pennies, Nickels, and Dimes

▶ **Nickels and Pennies**

Under the coins, write the total amount of money so far.
Then write the total using $. The first one is done for you.

6. 5¢ 5¢ 1¢

___5¢___ ___10¢___ ___11¢___ $ __0__ . __1__ __1__
                                              total

7. 5¢ 5¢ 1¢ 1¢ 1¢

_____ _____ _____ _____ _____ $ ___ . ___ ___
                                              total

8. 5¢ 5¢ 5¢ 1¢ 1¢

_____ _____ _____ _____ _____ $ ___ . ___ ___
                                              total

9. Maneka has 3 nickels and 6 pennies.

Draw the ⑤ s and ① s.

Write the total amount of money. $ ___ . ___ ___
                                              total

Name _____

▶ Dimes, Nickels, and Pennies

Under the coins, write the total amount of money so far.
Then write the total using $. The first one is done for you.

10. 10¢   5¢   1¢

   10¢   15¢   16¢ $ 0 . 1 6
   ____   ____   ____   total

---

11. 10¢   5¢   5¢   1¢   1¢

   ____   ____   ____   ____   ____ $ __ . __ __
                                                    total

---

12. 10¢   10¢   10¢   10¢   5¢   1¢

   ____   ____   ____   ____   ____   ____ $ __ . __ __
                                                    total

---

13. Cathy has 3 dimes, 4 nickels, and 2 pennies.

   Draw ⑩s, ⑤s, and ①s.

   Write the total amount of money. $ __ . __ __
                                                    total

Pennies, Nickels, and Dimes

Name _____

CA CC Content Standards **2.NBT.5**
Mathematical Practices **MP.1, MP.2, MP.5**

► PATH to FLUENCY **Add Within 100**

Add.

1.   36
   + 15

2.   64
   + 23

3.   13
   + 22

4.   47
   + 46

5.   60
   + 18

6.   11
   + 63

7.   28
   + 39

8.   76
   + 23

9.   33
   + 58

10.   63
   + 32

11.   44
   + 27

12.   45
   + 54

▶ PATH to FLUENCY **Add Within 100 (continued)**

Add.

13.
$$\begin{array}{r} 49 \\ + 51 \\ \hline \end{array}$$

14.
$$\begin{array}{r} 58 \\ + 26 \\ \hline \end{array}$$

15.
$$\begin{array}{r} 12 \\ + 85 \\ \hline \end{array}$$

16.
$$\begin{array}{r} 28 \\ + 31 \\ \hline \end{array}$$

17.
$$\begin{array}{r} 65 \\ + 16 \\ \hline \end{array}$$

18.
$$\begin{array}{r} 42 \\ + 26 \\ \hline \end{array}$$

19.
$$\begin{array}{r} 77 \\ + 19 \\ \hline \end{array}$$

20.
$$\begin{array}{r} 27 \\ + 53 \\ \hline \end{array}$$

21.
$$\begin{array}{r} 35 \\ + 40 \\ \hline \end{array}$$

22.
$$\begin{array}{r} 33 \\ + 67 \\ \hline \end{array}$$

23.
$$\begin{array}{r} 24 \\ + 19 \\ \hline \end{array}$$

24.
$$\begin{array}{r} 82 \\ + 7 \\ \hline \end{array}$$

Name _____

► **PATH to FLUENCY** *New Ten Challenge*

Work in 👥👥. Lay out Secret Code Cards like this.

10	60	1	6
1 0	**6 0**	**1**	**6**
20	70	2	7
2 0	**7 0**	**2**	**7**
30	80	3	8
3 0	**8 0**	**3**	**8**
40	90	4	9
4 0	**9 0**	**4**	**9**
50		5	
5 0		**5**	

1. 👤 Use Secret Code Cards to help you make a 2-digit addition (sum less than 100).

2. Make another 2-digit addition.

• Use the same tens cards.

• If 👤 *made a new ten,* use ones cards that *do not make a new ten.*

• If 👤 *did not make a new ten,* use ones cards that *make a new ten.*

Activity continues on next page.

▶ (PATH to FLUENCY) *New Ten Challenge* (continued)

2. Work together to check your work. Correct any errors.

3. Put the Secret Code Cards back. Switch roles and repeat. Continue until time is up.

*To play as a game and compete with another pair, use the **Scoring Rules** below.*

**Scoring Rules
for
*New Ten Challenge***

- Trade papers with another pair.
- Put a ✓ next to each correct answer.
  Put an X next to each incorrect answer.
- Give 1 point for each ✓.
  Subtract 3 points for each X.
- The pair with more points wins.

Fluency: Addition Within 100

► **Practice Adding Three Addends**

Add.

1. $15 + 29 + 36 =$ _____

2. $24 + 27 + 34 =$ _____

3. $36 + 33 + 39 =$ _____

4. $35 + 26 + 17 =$ _____

► **Practice Adding Four Addends**

Add.

5. $18 + 23 + 34 + 17 = $ _____

6. $38 + 32 + 14 + 25 = $ _____

7. $20 + 16 + 33 + 27 = $ _____

8. $26 + 41 + 35 + 12 = $ _____

Add Three or Four 2-Digit Addends

Name _____

CA CC Content Standards 2.OA.1, 2.NBT.2, 2.NBT.4, 2.NBT.5, 2.NBT.7, 2.MD.8
Mathematical Practices MP.1, MP.4, MP.5, MP.6

► Math and Recycling

To recycle means to use again. The second graders at Center School are collecting trash. They will recycle the trash to make musical instruments.

Collected So Far
102 water bottles
88 pie plates
63 paper towel rolls

Water Bottle
Maracas

Paper Towel
Roll Kazoo

Pie Plate
Tambourine

Solve each word problem.

1. Forty-eight children each want to make a pie plate tambourine. Each tambourine is made with 2 pie plates. Do they have enough pie plates?

   Circle yes or no.   yes   no

2. If they collect 10 more water bottles, how many water bottles will they have?

   ☐ _____
         label

3. If they collect 29 more paper towel rolls, will they have enough to make 75 kazoos?

   Circle yes or no.   yes   no

▶ Money for Cans and Bottles

Some states help people recycle by giving money back
when they return a bottle or can. This fleece jacket, this
yo-yo, and this park bench are all made from recycled
plastic bottles.

Solve each word problem.

4. Suzanne and Jing get 5 cents for each can or bottle
   they return. Suzanne returns 29 cans and 18 bottles.
   Jing returns 15 cans and 34 bottles. Who gets more
   money back?

   _____

5. Malia returns 12 bottles. She gets one nickel for each
   bottle. How much money does she get?

   _____

6. Roberto gets 5 cents for every can he returns.
   He gets $1.20. How many cans does he return?

   ☐ _____
        label

Focus on Mathematical Practices

1. Choose the ways that show 147.

   ○ one hundred seventy-four

   ○ 100 + 40 + 7

   ○

   ○ one hundred forty-seven

   ○ 100 + 70 + 4

2. Draw 124 using Quick Hundreds, Quick Tens, and circles. Write the number name. Then write the number in expanded form.

Name _____

Write a symbol from a tile to compare numbers.

| < | = | > |

3. 131 ◯ 124   4. 187 ◯ 187

5. 118 ◯ 128   6. 186 ◯ 168

Match each addition problem to its total on the right.

7.　　63
　　+ 25　　•　　　• 182

　　　48
　　+ 36　　•　　　• 88

94 + 11 •　　　• 84

85 + 97 •　　　• 105

8. Explain how you find the sum of 28 and 97.
   Then make a proof drawing.

```



```

Circle the correct sum.

9. $22 + 64 + 37 =$
| 87 |
| 113 |
| 123 |

10. $35 + 43 + 22 + 11 =$
| 101 |
| 111 |
| 113 |

Skip count by 5s.

11. 25 _____ _____ _____ _____ 55

Solve.

12. Sara has these coins. She has exactly enough
to buy a pencil. Under the coins, write the total
amount of money so far.

10¢   5¢   5¢   1¢   1¢

_____ _____ _____ _____ _____

What is the price of the pencil?
Use ¢ in your answer.

13. Scott has 44¢. List 3 different combinations
of coins that Scott could have.

[ ] dimes [ ] nickels [ ] pennies

[ ] dimes [ ] nickels [ ] pennies

[ ] dimes [ ] nickels [ ] pennies

14. Chris buys a folder that costs $1.23.
   She has these coins and bills. Circle the
   coins and bills Chris can use to buy the folder.

Write how much money Chris has left using $. $ ___ . ___ ___

---

15. Chen makes 38 red paper birds.
   He makes 25 yellow paper birds.
   How many paper birds does he make in all?
   Show two methods you can use to find the answer.

[ ] _____
         label

Family Letter

Content Overview

Dear Family:

Your child is working on a geometry and measurement unit. In this unit, children will use centimeter rulers to measure line segments and draw shapes.

You can help your child link geometry concepts learned in school with the real world. Encourage your child to find examples of different shapes (triangles, quadrilaterals including rectangles and squares, pentagons, and hexagons) in your home or neighborhood. This will help your child enjoy and understand geometry.

In Lesson 1 of this unit, your child will be asked to find the partner lengths of a line segment. An example is shown below.

If you have any questions or comments, please call or write to me. Thank you.

Sincerely,
Your child's teacher

CA CC

Unit 3 addresses the following standards from the *Common Core State Standards for Mathematics with California Additions*: **2.OA.2, 2.NBT.4, 2.NBT.5, 2.MD.1, 2.MD.2, 2.MD.3, 2.MD.4, 2.MD.9, 2.G.1**, and all Mathematical Practices.

© Houghton Mifflin Harcourt Publishing Company

Estimada familia:

Su niño está trabajando en una unidad que trata sobre geometría y medidas. En esta unidad los niños usarán reglas en centímetros para medir segmentos y trazar figuras.

Usted puede ayudar a su niño a relacionar los conceptos de geometría que aprenda en la escuela con el mundo real. Anímelo a buscar ejemplos de diferentes figuras (triángulos, cuadriláteros incluyendo rectángulos y cuadrados, pentágonos y hexágonos), en su casa o en el vecindario. Esto ayudará a su niño a disfrutar y a comprender la geometría.

En la Lección 1 de esta unidad se le pedirá a su niño que halle las partes de la longitud de un segmento. Abajo se muestra un ejemplo.

Partes	Partes de la longitud	Ecuaciones
1 y 5	6 cm / 1 cm / 5 cm	6 cm = 1 cm + 5 cm
2 y 4	2 cm / 4 cm	6 cm = 2 cm + 4 cm
3 y 3	3 cm / 3 cm	6 cm = 3 cm + 3 cm

Si tiene alguna pregunta o algún comentario, por favor comuníquese conmigo. Gracias.

Atentamente,
El maestro de su niño

CA CC

En la Unidad 3 se aplican los siguientes estándares auxiliares, contenidos en los *Estándares estatales comunes de matemáticas con adiciones para California*: **2.OA.2, 2.NBT.4, 2.NBT.5, 2.MD.1, 2.MD.2, 2.MD.3, 2.MD.4, 2.MD.9, 2.G.1** y todos los de prácticas matemáticas.

Name _____

CA CC Content Standards **2.MD.1, 2.MD.4**
Mathematical Practices **MP.1, MP.2, MP.3, MP.5, MP.6, MP.7**

▶ Count Centimeter Lengths

A **centimeter** is a unit of measure for **length**.
The short way to write centimeters is cm.

I cm

You can make a 6-cm **line segment** by pushing
together six 1-cm line lengths.

You can mark the 1-cm lengths.

To find the measure of the line segment, count the
1-cm lengths.

Use a centimeter ruler to mark the 1-cm lengths.
Count the 1-cm lengths.

1. ————————— ☐ cm

2. ————————————————————— ☐ cm

3. ———————————————— ☐ cm

4. ——————————————————————— ☐ cm

► **Draw Line Segments**

You can use a ruler to draw a **line segment** 7 cm long. Begin drawing at the zero edge of your ruler. Stop when you have counted seven 1-cm lengths.

Use your centimeter ruler to draw a **horizontal** line segment with the length given. Mark off and count 1-cm lengths to check the length.

5. 8 cm

6. 5 cm

7. Draw a **vertical** line segment 3 cm long. Mark off and count 1-cm lengths to check the length.

▶ The Ruler as a Group of Lengths

You can think of a ruler as a group of line segments with different lengths.

8. Copy this group of line segments.

9. Next, draw the same group of line segments closer together.

10. Write the number of centimeters at the end of each line segment in Exercise 9.

11. Imagine that you drew the segments so close together that they were on top of each other. What would the segments start to look like?

_____

12. Place a centimeter ruler under your diagram. What do the numbers on the ruler mean?

_____

▶ Explore Partner Lengths

13. Show the **partner lengths** for a 6-cm line segment.

| **Partners** | **Partner Lengths** | **Equations** |

☐ and ☐ ————————————— 6 cm = ☐ cm + ☐ cm

☐ and ☐ ————————————— 6 cm = ☐ cm + ☐ cm

☐ and ☐ ————————————— 6 cm = ☐ cm + ☐ cm

14. How many different pairs of partner lengths does
the 6-cm line segment have?

_____ different pairs

Measure Length

Name _____

CA CC Content Standards **2.MD.1, 2.MD.4, 2.G.1**
Mathematical Practices **MP.2, MP.5, MP.6, MP.8**

VOCABULARY
square
angle
right angle

▶ Draw and Identify Squares

> A **square** is a shape with four equal sides and four **right angles**.

1. Use your centimeter ruler. Draw a square with sides that are each 3 cm long.

Look at these shapes.

2. Are any of these shapes squares? _____

3. How are the **angles** of these shapes different from the angles of squares?

   _____

4. How are the sides of these shapes different from the sides of squares?

   _____

5. Is this shape a square? Explain why or why not.

   _____

   _____

VOCABULARY
rectangle
opposite sides

▶ Draw and Identify Rectangles

A **rectangle** is a shape with **opposite sides** that are equal in length and four right angles.

6. Use your centimeter ruler to draw a rectangle that is 6 cm long and 3 cm wide.

Look at these shapes.

7. Are these shapes rectangles? Explain why or why not.

_____

_____

8. Is a square a rectangle? Explain why or why not.

_____

_____

_____

VOCABULARY
triangle

► Compare Lengths of Sides of Triangles

A **triangle** is a shape with three angles and three straight sides. All of these shapes are triangles.

9. Measure each side of Triangle A. What did you discover about the sides?

_____

_____

10. Measure each side of Triangle B. What did you discover about the sides?

_____

_____

11. Measure each side of Triangle C. What did you discover about the sides?

_____

_____

12. Draw a loop to show how much longer the longest side of Triangle C is than the shortest side. The longest side

of Triangle C is ☐ cm longer than its shortest side.

VOCABULARY
quadrilateral
pentagon
hexagon

▶ **Describe Shapes**

A **quadrilateral** is a shape with four sides. A **pentagon** is a shape with five sides. A **hexagon** is a shape with six sides.

13.

How many sides? _____
How many angles? _____
Loop the shape.
quadrilateral
square
hexagon

14.

How many sides? _____
How many angles? _____
Loop the shape.
quadrilateral
pentagon
triangle

15.

How many sides? _____
How many angles? _____
Loop the shape.
hexagon
triangle
rectangle

16.

How many sides? _____
How many angles? _____
Loop the shape.
rectangle
pentagon
quadrilateral

Recognize and Draw Shapes

Name _____

CA CC Content Standards **2.OA.2, 2.MD.1, 2.MD.3, 2.G.1**
Mathematical Practices **MP.1, MP.2, MP.6, MP.7**

► Estimate and Measure Around a Square

Find the distance around each square.

1.

____ cm + ____ cm + ____ cm + ____ cm

= ____ cm

2.

____ cm + ____ cm + ____ cm + ____ cm

= ____ cm

Estimate and then measure each side.

Then find the distance around the square.

3. a. Complete the table. Use a
       centimeter ruler to measure.

Side	Estimate	Measure
EF		
FG		
GH		
HE		

b. Find the distance around the square.

____ cm + ____ cm + ____ cm + ____ cm = ____ cm

► Estimate and Measure Around a Rectangle

Find the distance around each rectangle.

4.

_____ cm + _____ cm + _____ cm + _____ cm

= _____ cm

5.

_____ cm + _____ cm + _____ cm + _____ cm

= _____ cm

Estimate and then measure each side.

Then find the distance around the rectangle.

6. a. Complete the table. Use a
centimeter ruler to measure.

Side	Estimate	Measure
WX		
XY		
YZ		
ZW		

b. Find the distance around the rectangle.

_____ cm + _____ cm + _____ cm + _____ cm = _____ cm

► **Estimate and Measure**

Find the distance around each triangle.

1.

_____ cm + _____ cm + _____ cm

= _____ cm

2.

_____ cm + _____ cm + _____ cm

= _____ cm

Estimate and then measure each side.

Then find the distance around the triangle.

3. **a.** Complete the table.

Side	Estimate	Measure
HI		
IJ		
JH		

b. Find the distance around the triangle.

_____ cm + _____ cm + _____ cm = _____ cm

▶ **Estimate and Measure (continued)**

4. **a.** Complete the table.

Side	Estimate	Measure
LM		
MO		
OL		

b. Find the distance around the triangle.

_____ cm + _____ cm + _____ cm = _____ cm

5. **a.** Complete the table.

Side	Estimate	Measure
DE		
EF		
FD		

b. Find the distance around the triangle.

_____ cm + _____ cm + _____ cm = _____ cm

6. **a.** Complete the table.

Side	Estimate	Measure
PQ		
QR		
RP		

b. Find the distance around the triangle.

_____ cm + _____ cm + _____ cm = _____ cm

► **Rectangular Prisms**

Cut on solid lines.
Fold on dashed lines.

Rectangular Prisms

VOCABULARY
rectangular prism
views

► Build and Draw Rectangular Prisms

Using unit cubes, build a **rectangular prism** to match each description. Draw the rectangular prism from the top, front, and side **views**.

1. two rows of three unit cubes.

      top view   **front view**   **side view**

2. one row of two unit cubes stacked on top of another row of two unit cubes.

      top view   **front view**   **side view**

► Build Rectangular Prisms from Drawings

Build a rectangular prism to match each set of views.

3.   **top view**   **front view**   **side view**

4.   **top view**   **front view**   **side view**

► **Identify Shapes**

A	B	C
D	E	F
G	H	I
J	K	L

Draw Using Faces

Family Letter

Content Overview

Dear Family:

In this unit, your child will be collecting measurement data and using that data to make line plots. A *line plot* is a display that uses a number line and dots (or other marks) to represent data. For this reason, line plots are sometimes called *dot plots*.

Your child will be asked to bring one or two pencils to school. The length of each pencil should be more than 1 inch and less than 8 inches. Children will work in small groups. They will measure each pencil brought in by the members of their group and then make a line plot similar to the one shown below.

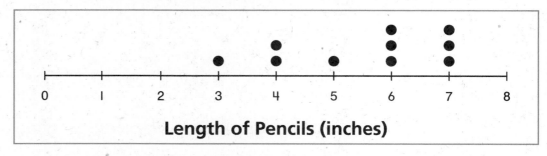

Length of Pencils (inches)

In this unit, your child will also be given several experiences that will help build understanding that the smaller the unit used to measure a given length or distance, the more of those units will be needed.

So, for example, since centimeters are shorter than inches, when the paintbrush below is measured in both centimeters and inches, the number of centimeters is more than the number of inches.

Sincerely,
Your child's teacher

CA CC

Unit 3 addresses the following standards from the *Common Core State Standards for Mathematics with California Additions*: **2.OA.2, 2.NBT.4, 2.NBT.5, 2.MD.1, 2.MD.2, 2.MD.3, 2.MD.4, 2.MD.9, 2.G.1**, and all Mathematical Practices.

© Houghton Mifflin Harcourt Publishing Company

Carta a la familia

Un vistazo general al contenido

Estimada familia:

En esta unidad, su niño reunirá datos sobre medidas y usará esos datos para hacer diagramas de puntos. Un *diagrama de puntos* es un diagrama que usa una recta numérica y puntos u otras marcas para representar datos.

Se le pedirá a su niño que traiga uno o dos lápices a la escuela. Cada lápiz debe medir más de 1 pulgada de longitud pero menos de 8. Los niños trabajarán en grupos pequeños. Medirán los lápices de cada miembro de su grupo y luego, harán un diagrama de puntos como el que se muestra debajo.

Longitud de los lápices (pulgadas)

También en esta unidad, a su niño se le brindarán diversas experiencias que lo ayudarán a comprender que entre más pequeña sea la unidad que se use para medir una determinada longitud o distancia, más de esas unidades se necesitarán.

Entonces, por ejemplo, como los centímetros son más cortos que las pulgadas, cuando el pincel de abajo se mide en centímetros y en pulgadas, el número de centímetros es mayor que el número de pulgadas.

Atentamente,
El maestro de su niño

CA CC

En la Unidad 3 se aplican los siguientes estándares auxiliares, contenidos en los *Estándares estatales comunes de matemáticas con adiciones para California*: 2.OA.2, 2.NBT.4, 2.NBT.5, 2.MD.1, 2.MD.2, 2.MD.3, 2.MD.4, 2.MD.9, 2.G.1 y todos los de prácticas matemáticas.

© Houghton Mifflin Harcourt Publishing Company

25 ↑	50 ↑	75 ↑	100 ↑
24	49	74	99
23	48	73	98
22	47	72	97
21	46	71	96
20	45	70	95
19	44	69	94
18	43	68	93
17	42	67	92
16	41	66	91
15	40	65	90
14	39	64	89
13	38	63	88
12	37	62	87
11	36	61	86
10	35	60	85
9	34	59	84
8	33	58	83
7	32	57	82
6	31	56	81
5	30	55	80
4	29	54	79
3	28	53	78
2	27	52	77
1	26	51	76
	25 ↓	50 ↓	75 ↓

Side labels: 50, 100, 20, 70, 10, 40, 30, 60, 90, 80

Step 1: Cut out on the dashed lines.

Step 2: Put the sections in order.

Step 3: Tape or paste the sections together.

← 100

← 76
← 74
Tape or paste

← 51
← 49
Tape or paste

← 26
← 24
Tape or paste

← 1

Meter Tape (Vertical) **135**

Estimate and Measure with Centimeters

CA CC Content Standards **2.NBT.4, 2.MD.1, 2.MD.3, 2.MD.4, 2.MD.9**
Mathematical Practices **MP.1, MP.4, MP.5, MP.6, MP.7**

► Estimate and Measure

Find a part of your hand that is about each length.

1. I cm _____

2. I0 cm _____

Find a part of your body that is about I meter long.

3. I m _____

Find the real object. Estimate and measure its length.
Choose the nearest centimeter endpoint.

4.

Estimate: about _____ cm

Measure: _____ cm

5.

Estimate: about _____ cm

Measure: _____ cm

6.

Estimate: about _____ cm

Measure: _____ cm

7.

Estimate: about _____ m

Measure: _____ m

Draw a line segment to show each length.

8. I cm

9. I0 cm

▶ Measure Heights

When you measure a length greater than 1 meter, you place two meter sticks end to end. The first meter stick is 100 cm. You add 100 to the number of centimeters you read from the second meter stick.

10. Complete the table for each person in your group.

Person's Name	Estimated Height (cm)	Actual Height (cm)	Difference Between Estimated and Actual Height (cm)

Use the table you collected to answer these questions.

11. Who is the tallest person in your group?

    _____

12. How much taller is the tallest person than the shortest person? Measure this difference and check by adding. _____

13. Whose estimated height was closest to his or her actual height? _____

14. On a separate sheet of paper, use the table to write four more questions. Trade your questions with another group and answer each other's questions.

VOCABULARY
line plot

▶ Introduce Line Plots

Look at this **line plot**.

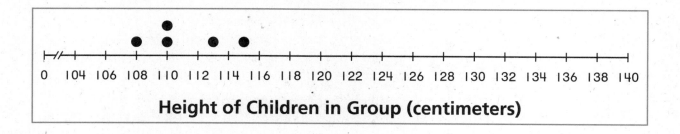

Height of Children in Group (centimeters)

▶ Make a Line Plot

15. Draw dots for the heights of the children in your
group. Use data from the table on page 138.

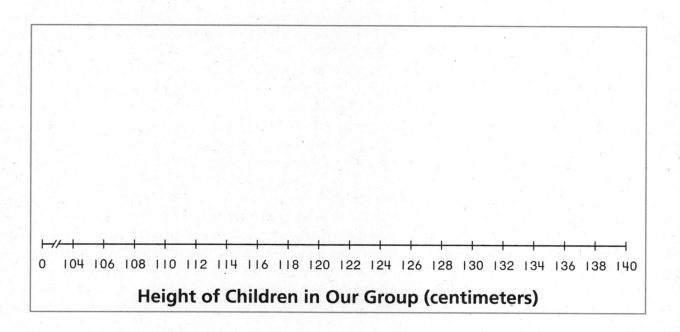

Height of Children in Our Group (centimeters)

▶ Discuss a Line Plot

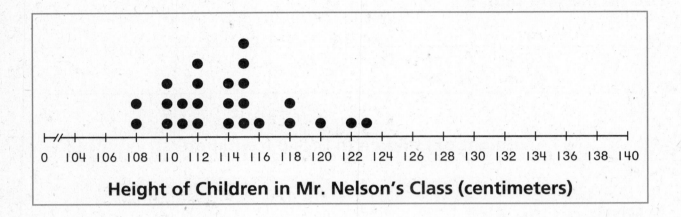

Height of Children in Mr. Nelson's Class (centimeters)

▶ Show Class Data on a Line Plot

16. Draw dots for the heights of the children in your class.

Height of Children in Class (centimeters)

Estimate and Measure with Centimeters

Name _____

CA CC Content Standards 2.MD.1, 2.MD.2, 2.MD.3, 2.MD.9
Mathematical Practices MP.2, MP.5, MP.6, MP.7, MP.8

▶ Make an Inch Ruler

Directions:

Step 1: Cut along the dashed lines.

Step 2: Place the sections in the correct order.

Step 3: Tape or glue together the sections at the tab.

Step 4: Write a **6** where the two strips meet.

TAB

5

4

3

2

1

0

12

11

10

9

8

7

TAB

5

4

3

2

—

0

12

11

10

9

8

7

Inch Ruler

VOCABULARY
inch (in.)

▶ Measure to the Nearest Inch

To measure to the nearest **inch (in.)**, place the zero mark on your ruler at the left end of the object. Find the inch mark that is closest to the right end of the object.

To the nearest inch, the length of this toy car is 2 inches.
Measure the length of each object to the nearest inch.

1. _____

2. _____

3. _____

4. Draw a horizontal line segment that is 2 in. long.

5. Draw a horizontal line segment that is 6 in. long.

► Estimate and Measure in Inches

6. Describe a part of your hand that measures about 2 in.

   _____

7. Describe a part of your hand that measures about 1 in.

   _____

8. Describe a part of your hand that measures about 6 in.

   _____

Estimate and measure the length of each line segment.

9. |————————————————|

   Estimated length: _____ Measured length: _____

10. |————————————————————|

   Estimated length: _____ Measured length: _____

11. Find four classroom objects that you can measure in inches and then in centimeters. Choose two objects with a length between 12 inches and 24 inches. Complete the table.

Object	Estimated length (in.)	Measured length (in.)	Measured length (cm)

Estimate and Measure with Inches

► **Make a Yardstick**

Directions:

> **Step 1:** Cut along the dashed lines.
>
> **Step 2:** Place the sections in the correct order.
>
> **Step 3:** Tape or glue together the sections at the tab.

TAB	TAB	TAB	TAB	TAB	
	1 ft		2 ft		36 3 ft
— 5	— 11	— 17	— 23	— 29	— 35
— 4	— 10	— 16	— 22	— 28	— 34
— 3	— 9	— 15	— 21	— 27	— 33
— 2	— 8	— 14	— 20	— 26	— 32
— 1	— 7	— 13	— 19	— 25	— 31
	↙ 6		↙ 18		↙ 30
— 0					

Yardstick

VOCABULARY
foot (ft)
yard (yd)

▶ Measure in Feet and Yards

Find each length to the nearest **foot (ft)**.

12. width of your desk

_____

13. length from your knee to your ankle

_____

Find each length to the nearest **yard (yd)**.

14. height of the classroom door

_____

15. length of a bookshelf

_____

Measure each length to the nearest foot and to the nearest yard.

16. width of the classroom door

_____ ft

_____ yd

17. length of the classroom board

_____ ft

_____ yd

18. What do you notice about the numbers when you measure in yards instead of feet? Why?

_____

_____

▶ Estimate and Measure Height

Estimate your height in inches. Then work with a partner to find your actual height.

19. Estimate: _____

20. Actual height: _____

▶ Height in Centimeters and Inches

Draw a dot to show your height in centimeters.

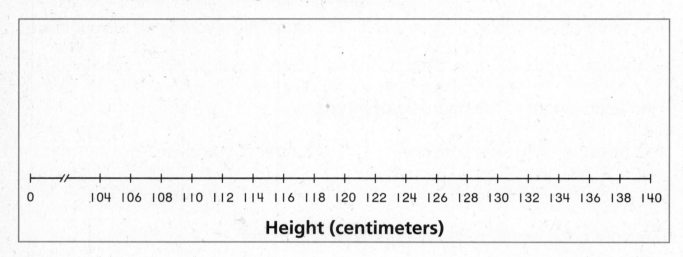

Height (centimeters)

Draw a dot to show your height in inches.

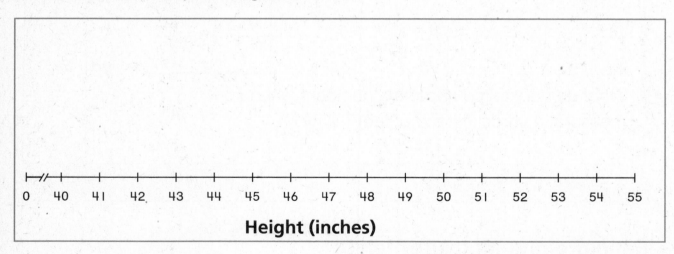

Height (inches)

3-8

Class Activity

Name

CA CC Content Standards **2.MD.1, 2.MD.2, 2.MD.3, 2.MD.9**
Mathematical Practices **MP.2, MP.4, MP.5, MP.6, MP.7, MP.8**

▶ Lengths of Pencils

▶ Width of Books

Width of Books (inches)

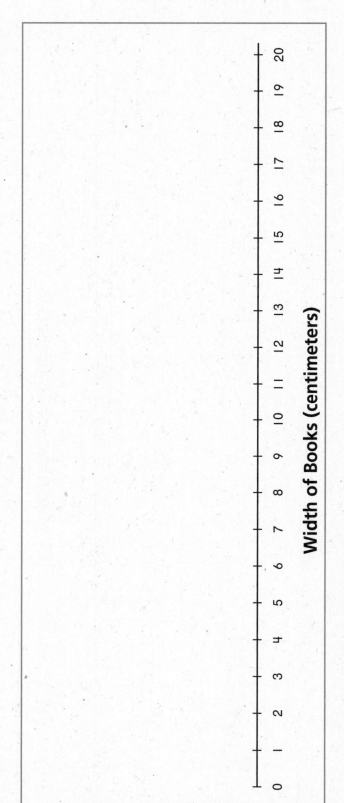

Width of Books (centimeters)

► **Measurement Data on Line Plots**

Length (inches)

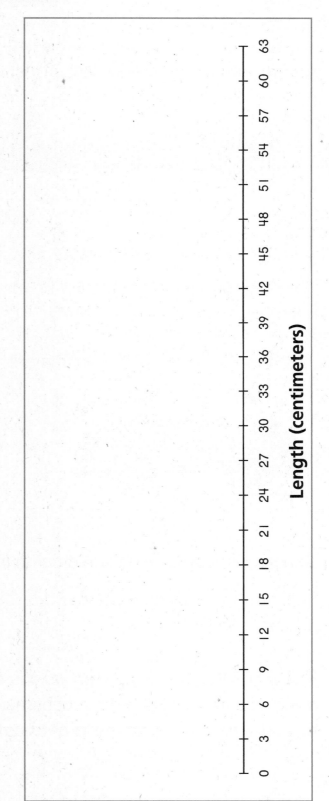

Length (centimeters)

Name _____

▶ Compare Measurement Units

Ring *more* or *less*.

---

1. Arul measures the celery stick in inches.

6 inches

Liam measures the same celery stick in centimeters.

The number of centimeters will be *more less* than the number of inches.

---

2. Jael measures the car in centimeters.

6 centimeters

Desmond measures the same car in inches.

The number of inches will be *more less* than the number of centimeters.

---

3. Rue measures a carrot in inches and Peter measures the same carrot in centimeters. Whose measurement will have the larger number of units?

_____

Name _____

CA CC Content Standards **2.MD.1, 2.G.1**
Mathematical Practices **MP.1, MP.4, MP.5, MP.6**

▶ Math and Quilts

A patchwork quilt is made by sewing pieces of cloth together. Look for shapes in these patchwork quilts.

1. Color each shape a different color.

Shape	triangle	quadrilateral	pentagon	hexagon
Color	red	orange	blue	yellow

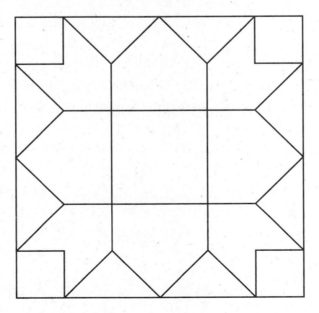

► Make Quilts

2. Continue the pattern to complete this quilt square.

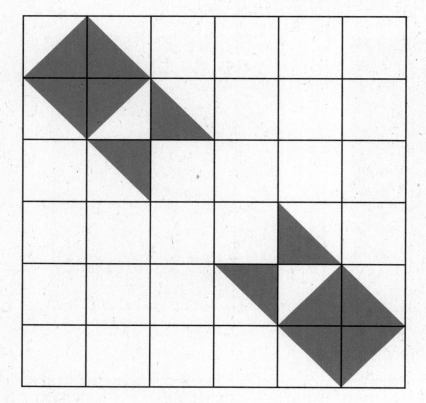

3. Use centimeter grid paper. Draw a square that is 16 centimeters long on each side. Use your square to make a quilt pattern. Color your quilt square.

When you finish, count the shapes.

_____ triangles   _____ quadrilaterals

_____ pentagons   _____ hexagons

Measure each string to the nearest centimeter.
Then match the string to its length.

1. [string]   •   • 6 cm

2.   •   • 2 cm

3. [string]   •   • 3 cm

4.   •   • 5 cm

5. [string]   •   • 4 cm

---

6. Show the lengths of the five strings on this line plot.

   0   1   2   3   4   5   6   7   8

Lengths of Strings (centimeters)

How many strings are longer than 3 cm?

[ ] strings

7. Estimate the length of the eraser in inches.

Write your estimate.

about ☐ _____
label

Measure the eraser to the nearest inch.
Circle the actual measure.

The eraser is
| 3 |
| 4 |
| 5 |
inches long.

8. Measure each pencil in inches.

☐ inches

☐ inches

Is the sentence true? Choose Yes or No.

The yellow pencil is 2 inches longer than the blue pencil.	○ Yes	○ No
The yellow pencil is 1 inch longer than the blue pencil.	○ Yes	○ No
The blue pencil is 2 inches shorter than the yellow pencil.	○ Yes	○ No

9. Draw each shape in the correct box below.

Has exactly 6 sides	Has exactly 4 angles	Has less than 4 angles

10. Measure the crayon in centimeters and in inches.

Circle the number or words in each box that makes the sentence true.

The crayon is | 8 9 10 | centimeters long.

The crayon is | 3 4 5 | inches long.

There are fewer | inches than centimeters / centimeters than inches | because | inches are bigger than centimeters. / centimeters are bigger than inches. |

Name _____

Name the shapes using the words on the tiles.

| cube | pentagon | triangle | hexagon | quadrilateral |

11.

12.

13.

14.

_____ _____ _____ _____

_____

15. Complete the table. Use an inch ruler to measure.

Side	Estimate	Measure
EF		
FG		
GH		
HE		

Find the distance around
the square. Show your work.

The distance round the square is ⬜ inches.

Problem Types

	Result Unknown	Change Unknown	Start Unknown
Add To	Aisha has 46 stamps in her collection. Then her grandfather gives her 29 stamps. How many stamps does she have now? *Situation and Solution Equation*[1]: $46 + 29 = \square$	Aisha has 46 stamps in her collection. Then her grandfather gives her some stamps. Now she has 75 stamps. How many stamps did her grandfather give her? *Situation Equation:* $46 + \square = 75$ *Solution Equation:* $\square = 75 - 46$	Aisha has some stamps in her collection. Then her grandfather gives her 29 stamps. Now she has 75 stamps. How many stamps did she have to start? *Situation Equation:* $\square + 29 = 75$ *Solution Equation:* $\square = 75 - 29$
Take From	A store has 43 bottles of water at the start of the day. During the day, the store sells 25 bottles. How many bottles do they have at the end of the day? *Situation and Solution Equation:* $43 - 25 = \square$	A store has 43 bottles of water at the start of the day. The store has 18 bottles left at the end of the day. How many bottles does the store sell? *Situation Equation:* $43 - \square = 18$ *Solution Equation:* $\square = 43 - 18$	A store sells 25 bottles of water during one day. At the end of the day 18 bottles are left. How many bottles did the store have at the beginning of the day? *Situation Equation:* $\square - 25 = 18$ *Solution Equation:* $\square = 25 + 18$

[1]A situation equation represents the structure (action) in the problem situation. A solution equation shows the operation used to find the answer.

Problem Types continued

Problem Types (continued)

	Total Unknown	Addend Unknown	Both Addends Unknown
Put Together/ Take Apart	A clothing store has 39 shirts with short sleeves and 45 shirts with long sleeves. How many shirts does the store have in all? *Math Drawing²:* [diagram: box at top, branching to 39 and 45] *Situation and Solution Equation:* $39 + 45 = \square$	Of the 84 shirts in a clothing store, 39 have short sleeves. The rest have long sleeves. How many shirts have long sleeves? *Math Drawing:* [diagram: 84 at top, branching to 39 and box] *Situation Equation:* $84 = 39 + \square$ *Solution Equation:* $84 - 39 = \square$	Pam has 24 roses. How many can she put in her red vase and how many in her blue vase? *Math Drawing:* [diagram: 24 at top, branching to two boxes] *Situation Equation:* $24 = \square + \square$

²These math drawings are called Math Mountains in Grades 1–3 and break-apart drawings in Grades 4 and 5.

	Difference Unknown	Greater Unknown	Smaller Unknown
Compare[1]	Alex has 64 trading cards. Lucy has 48 trading cards. How many **more** trading cards does **Alex** have than Lucy? Lucy has 48 trading cards. Alex has 64 trading cards. How many **fewer** trading cards does **Lucy** have than Alex? *Math Drawing:* A [64] L [48] (?) *Situation Equation:* $48 + \square = 64$ or $\square = 64 - 48$ *Solution Equation:* $\square = 64 - 48$	**Leading Language** Lucy has 48 trading cards. **Alex** has **16 more** trading cards than Lucy. How many trading cards does Alex have? **Misleading Language** Lucy has 48 trading cards. **Lucy** has **16 fewer** trading cards than Alex. How many trading cards does Alex have? *Math Drawing:* A [?] L [48] (16) *Situation and Solution Equation:* $48 + 16 = \square$	**Leading Language** Alex has 64 trading cards. **Lucy** has **16 fewer** trading cards than Alex. How many trading cards does Lucy have? **Misleading Language** Alex has 64 trading cards. **Alex** has **16 more** trading cards than Lucy. How many trading cards does Lucy have? *Math Drawing:* A [64] L [?] (16) *Situation Equation:* $\square + 16 = 64$ or $\square = 64 - 16$ *Solution Equation:* $\square = 64 - 16$

[1]A comparison sentence can always be said in two ways. One way uses *more*, and the other uses *fewer* or *less*. Misleading language suggests the wrong operation. For example, it says *Lucy has 16 fewer trading cards than Alex*, but you have to add 16 cards to the number of cards Lucy has to get the number of cards Alex has.

Glossary

5-groups

||||| ||||| tens in 5-groups

OOOOO
OOOOO   ones in 5-groups

A

add

●●●●   ●●

$4 + 2 = 6$

addend

$5 + 6 = 11$

↑   ↑

addends

Adding Up Method (for Subtraction)

$$\begin{array}{r} 144 \\ -\ 68 \\ \hline 76 \end{array}$$

$68 + 2 = 70$
$70 + 30 = 100$
$100 + 44 = 144$

$\boxed{76}$

addition doubles

Both addends (or partners) are the same.

$4 + 4 = 8$

A.M.

Use A.M. for times between midnight and noon.

analog clock

angle

These are angles.

array

This rectangular array has 3 rows and 5 columns.

bar graph

Coins in My Collection

horizontal bar graph

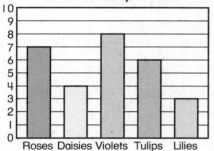

Flowers in My Garden

vertical bar graph

break-apart

You can break apart a larger number to get two smaller amounts called break-aparts.

10

6   4

break-aparts of 10

cent

front   back

1 cent or 1¢ or $0.01

centimeter (cm)

cent sign

56¢

↑

cent sign

clock

analog clock

digital clock

12:30

column

This rectangular array has 4 columns with 3 tiles in each column.

compare numbers

Compare numbers using >, <, or =.

$52 > 25$

$25 < 52$

$25 = 25$

comparison bars

You can add labels and fill in numbers to help you solve *Compare* problems.

count all

$5 + 3 = \square$

1 2 3 4 5 6 7 8

$5 + 3 = \boxed{8}$

count on

$5 + 3 = \boxed{8}$

$5 + \boxed{3} = 8$

$8 - 5 = \boxed{3}$

Already **5**

cube

D

data

	Sisters	Brothers
Kendra	2	1
Scott	2	0
Ida	0	1

data

The data in the table show how many sisters and how many brothers each child has.

decade numbers

10, 20, 30, 40, 50, 60, 70, 80, 90

decimal point

$4.25

decimal point

diagonal

diagonal

difference

$$11 - 3 = 8$$

difference ⟶ $\begin{array}{r} 11 \\ -\ 3 \\ \hline 8 \end{array}$

digital clock

12:30

digits

0, 1, 2, 3, 4, 5, 6, 7, 8, 9

15 is a 2-digit number.

The 1 in 15 means 1 ten.

The 5 in 15 means 5 ones.

dime

front   back

10 cents or 10¢ or $0.10

dollar

100 cents or

100¢ or $1.00

front

back

dollar sign

$4.25

↑

dollar sign

doubles minus 1

7 + 7 = 14, so

7 + 6 = 13, 1 less than 14.

doubles minus 2

7 + 7 = 14, so

7 + 5 = 12, 2 less than 14.

doubles plus 1

6 + 6 = 12, so

6 + 7 = 13, 1 more than 12.

doubles plus 2

6 + 6 = 12, so

6 + 8 = 14, 2 more than 12.

E

equal shares

2 halves   4 fourths

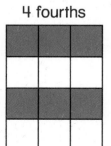

equal to (=)

$$5 + 3 = 8$$

5 plus 3 is equal to 8.

equation

$$4 + 3 = 7 \qquad 7 = 4 + 3$$
$$9 - 5 = 4 \qquad 4 + 5 = 8 + 1$$

An equation must have an = sign.

equation chain

$$3 + 4 = 5 + 2 = 8 - 1 = 7$$

estimate

Make a reasonable guess about how many or how much.

even number

A number is even if you can make groups of 2 and have none left over.

8 is an even number.

exact change

I will pay with 4 dimes and 3 pennies. That is the exact change. I won't get any money back.

expanded form

$$283 = 200 + 80 + 3$$

Expanded Method (for Addition)

$$
\begin{array}{r}
78 = 70 + 8 \\
+\,57 = 50 + 7 \\
\hline
120 + 15 = 135
\end{array}
$$

Expanded Method (for Subtraction)

$$
\begin{array}{r}
64 = \overset{50}{\cancel{60}} + \overset{14}{\cancel{4}} \\
-\,28 = 20 + 8 \\
\hline
30 + 6 = 36
\end{array}
$$

extra information

Franny has 8 kittens and 2 dogs. 4 kittens are asleep. How many kittens are awake?

$$8 - 4 = \boxed{4}$$

The number of dogs is extra information. It is not needed to solve the problem.

fewer

There are fewer ▢ than △.

foot (ft)

foot

12 inches = 1 foot   (not drawn to scale)

fourth

square

The picture shows 4 fourths. A fourth of the square is shaded.

G

greater than (>)

34   >   25

34 is greater than 25.

greatest

25   41   63

63 is the greatest number.

group name

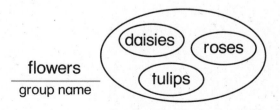

flowers
group name

H

half

square

The picture shows 2 halves. A half of the square is shaded.

half hour

5 minutes
10 minutes
15 minutes
20 minutes
25 minutes
30 minutes

30 minutes = 1 half hour

hexagon

A hexagon has 6 sides and 6 angles.

hidden information

Heather bought a dozen eggs. She used 7 of them to make breakfast. How many eggs does she have left?

$$12 - 7 = \boxed{5}$$

The hidden information is that a dozen means 12.

horizontal

$$4 + 5 = 9$$

horizontal form   horizontal line

horizontal bar graph

Coins in My Collection

hour

60 minutes = 1 hour

hour hand

hour hand

hundreds

3 hundreds

347 has 3 hundreds.

hundreds

I

inch (in.)

1 inch

L

least

14   7   63

7 is the least number.

length

The length of the pencil is about 17 cm.
(not to scale)

less than (<)

45 < 46

45 is less than 46.

line plot

line segment

M

make a ten

$8 + 6 = \square$

8 • • | • • • •

10 + 4
10 + 4 = 14,
so 8 + 6 = 14

matching drawing

○○○   fewer
○○○○○○   more

Math Mountain

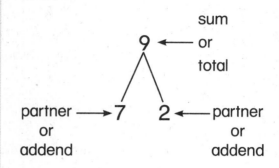

meter(m)

100 centimeters = 1 meter
(not drawn to scale)

minus

8 − 3 = 5

8 minus 3 equals 5.

$$\begin{array}{r} 8 \\ -\,3 \\ \hline 5 \end{array}$$

minute

60 seconds = 1 minute

© Houghton Mifflin Harcourt Publishing Company

Glossary (continued)

minute hand

minute hand: points to the minutes

more

There are more ⬭ than ☐.

N

New Groups Above Method

$$\begin{array}{r} {\scriptstyle 1} \\ 56 \\ +\ 28 \\ \hline 84 \end{array}$$

$6 + 8 = 14$

The 1 new ten in 14 goes up to the tens place.

New Groups Below Method

$$\begin{array}{r} 56 \\ +\ 28 \\ \hline {\scriptstyle 1} \\ 84 \end{array}$$

$6 + 8 = 14$

The 1 new ten in 14 goes below in the tens place.

nickel

front   back

5 cents or 5¢ or $0.05

not equal to (≠)

$6 + 4 \neq 8$

$6 + 4$ is not equal to 8.

number line diagram

0 1 2 3 4 5 6 7 8 9 10

This is a number line diagram.

number name

12

twelve ← number name

O

odd number

A number is odd if you can make groups of 2 and have one left over.

9 is an odd number.

ones

7 ones

347 has 7 ones.

↑
ones

© Houghton Mifflin Harcourt Publishing Company

opposite operations

Addition and subtraction are opposite operations.

$$5 + 9 = 14$$
$$14 - 9 = 5$$

Use addition to check subtraction. Use subtraction to check addition.

opposite sides

opposite sides

order

2, 5, 6

The numbers 2, 5, and 6 are in order from least to greatest.

P

pair

A group of 2 is a pair.

The picture shows 4 pairs of counters.

partner lengths

partner lengths of 4 cm

4 cm

1 cm   3 cm

2 cm   2 cm

partners

$$9 + 6 = 15$$

partners (addends)

penny

front   back

1 cent or 1¢ or $0.01

pentagon

A pentagon has 5 sides and 5 angles.

Glossary (continued)

picture graph

| Flowers | |
| Vases | |

plus

$3 + 2 = 5$

$$\begin{array}{r} 3 \\ +2 \\ \hline 5 \end{array}$$

3 plus 2 equals 5.

P.M.

Use P.M. for times between noon and midnight.

proof drawing

$86 + 57 = 143$

Q

quadrilateral

A quadrilateral has 4 sides and 4 angles.

quarter

front   back

25 cents or 25¢ or $0.25

A quarter is another name for a fourth.

A quarter is a fourth of a dollar.

quick hundreds

347

quick hundreds

quick tens

162

quick tens

R

rectangle

A rectangle has 4 sides and 4 right angles.

Opposite sides have the same length.

rectangular prism

right angle

right angle

A right angle is sometimes called a *square corner*.

round

Express a number to the nearest ten or hundred. You can round down or round up.

$$52 \longrightarrow 50 \qquad 278 \longrightarrow 300$$

row

This rectangular array has 3 rows with 4 tiles in each row.

ruler

A ruler is used to measure length.

scale

The numbers along the side or the bottom of a graph.

Show All Totals Method

$$
\begin{array}{r}
25 \\
+\,48 \\
\hline
60 \\
13 \\
\hline
73
\end{array}
\qquad
\begin{array}{r}
724 \\
+\,158 \\
\hline
800 \\
70 \\
12 \\
\hline
882
\end{array}
$$

situation equation

A baker baked 100 loaves of bread. He sold some loaves. There are 73 loaves left. How many loaves of bread did he sell?

$$100 - \boxed{} = 73$$

situation equation

Glossary (continued)

skip count

skip count by 2s: 2, 4, 6, 8, . . .
skip count by 5s: 5, 10, 15, 20, . . .
skip count by 10s: 10, 20, 30, 40, 50, . . .

solution equation

A baker baked 100 loaves of bread. He sold some loaves. There are 73 loaves left. How many loaves of bread did he sell?

$$100 - 73 = \boxed{}$$

solution equation

square

A square has 4 equal sides and 4 right angles.

subtract

8 − 5 = 3

subtraction doubles

Both addends or partners are the same.
8 − 4 = 4

sum

$$4 + 3 = 7$$

$$\begin{array}{r} 4 \\ + 3 \\ \hline 7 \end{array}$$

sum ⟶

survey

When you collect data by asking people questions, you are taking a survey.

teen number

any number from 11 to 19

11 12 13 14 15 16 17 18 19

tens

□ □ □ |||| o o o o o
              o o

4 tens

347 has 4 tens.

↑
tens

third

square

The picture shows 3 thirds. A third of the square is shaded.

thousand

1,000 = ten hundreds

total

$$10 \leftarrow total$$

$$8 \quad 2$$

triangle

A triangle has 3 sides and 3 angles.

U

ungroup

Ungroup when you need more ones or tens to subtract.

Ungroup First Method

$$\begin{array}{r} 6\,4 \\ -2\,8 \\ \hline \uparrow \quad \uparrow \\ yes \; no \end{array}$$

1. Check to see if there are enough tens and ones to subtract.

$$\begin{array}{r} 5\,14 \\ \cancel{6}\cancel{4} \\ -2\,8 \\ \hline \end{array}$$

2. You can get more ones by taking from the tens and putting them in the ones place.

$$\begin{array}{r} 5\,14 \\ \cancel{6}\cancel{4} \\ -2\,8 \\ \hline 3\,6 \end{array}$$

3. Subtract from either right to left or left to right.

unknown addend

$$3 + \boxed{} = 9$$

unknown addend

unknown total

$$3 + 6 = \boxed{}$$

unknown total

V

vertical

$$\begin{array}{r} 4 \\ +3 \\ \hline 7 \end{array}$$

vertical form   vertical line

vertical bar graph

Flowers in My Garden

view

This is the side view of the rectangular prism above.

W

width

width or length

length width

Y

yard (yd)

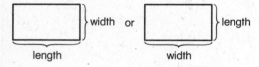

3 feet = 1 yard (not drawn to scale)

California Common Core Standards for Mathematical Content

2.OA Operations and Algebraic Thinking

Represent and solve problems involving addition and subtraction.

2.OA.1	Use addition and subtraction within 100 to solve one- and two-step word problems involving situations of adding to, taking from, putting together, taking apart, and comparing, with unknowns in all positions, e.g., by using drawings and equations with a symbol for the unknown number to represent the problem.	Unit 1 Lessons 1, 2, 4, 10, 11, 12, 13, 14, 15, 16, 17, 18, 19, 20, 21; Unit 2 Lessons 1, 2, 7, 15; Unit 4 Lessons 3, 4, 5, 12, 13, 14, 16, 17, 18, 19, 20, 21, 22, 23; Unit 5 Lessons 3, 4, 5, 6, 7, 9, 10; Unit 6 Lessons 8, 9, 14, 15; Unit 7 Lessons 3, 4, 5 **Daily Routine:** Money Routine

Add and subtract within 20.

2.OA.2	Fluently add and subtract within 20 using mental strategies. By end of Grade 2, know from memory all sums of two one-digit numbers.	Unit 1 Lessons 1, 2, 3, 4, 5, 7, 8, 9, 10, 11, 12, 13, 14, 15, 16, 17, 18, 19, 20, 21; Unit 2 Lessons 1, 2, 6; Unit 3 Lessons 1, 2, 3, 4; Unit 4 Lessons 6, 13; Unit 5 Lessons 3, 4, 5, 9, 10 **Quick Practices:** Unknown Addend; Stay or Go?; Equation Chains; Blue Math Mountain Cards; Dive the Deep; Make-a-Ten Cards: Addition; Make-a-Ten Cards: Subtraction; Addition Sprint; Subtraction Sprint; Teen Addition Flash; Teen Subtraction Flash

Work with equal groups of objects to gain foundations for multiplication.

2.OA.3	Determine whether a group of objects (up to 20) has an odd or even number of members, e.g., by pairing objects or counting them by 2s; write an equation to express an even number as a sum of two equal addends.	Unit 1 Lessons 6, 7, 21; Unit 7 Lesson 1 **Quick Practices:** Count by 2s, Even or Odd?
2.OA.4	Use addition to find the total number of objects arranged in rectangular arrays with up to 5 rows and up to 5 columns; write an equation to express the total as a sum of equal addends.	Unit 7 Lessons 1, 6

2.NBT Number and Operations in Base Ten

Understand place value.

2.NBT.1	Understand that the three digits of a three-digit number represent amounts of hundreds, tens, and ones; e.g., 706 equals 7 hundreds, 0 tens, and 6 ones.	Unit 2 Lessons 1, 2, 3, 4, 5, 6, 7, 8, 9, 10, 11; Unit 4 Lessons 7, 8, 9, 10, 12 ,14; Unit 6 Lesson 2 **Daily Routines:** Comparing 2-Digit Numbers, Comparing 3-Digit Numbers **Quick Practices:** Tens Talking; Unscramble the Hundreds, Tens, and Ones

2.NBT.1a	Understand that the three digits of a three-digit number represent amounts of hundreds, tens, and ones; e.g., 706 equals 7 hundreds, 0 tens, and 6 ones. Understand the following as special cases: a. 100 can be thought of as a bundle of ten tens—called a "hundred."	Unit 2 Lessons 1, 2, 3, 4, 6, 7, 8, 9, 11; Unit 4 Lessons 3, 4, 7, 8, 9, 10, 12, 14; Unit 6 Lessons 1, 4 **Quick Practice:** Tens Talking
2.NBT.1b	Understand that the three digits of a three-digit number represent amounts of hundreds, tens, and ones; e.g., 706 equals 7 hundreds, 0 tens, and 6 ones. Understand the following as special cases: b. The numbers 100, 200, 300, 400, 500, 600, 700, 800, 900 refer to one, two, three, four, five, six, seven, eight, or nine hundreds (and 0 tens and 0 ones).	Unit 4 Lesson 7; Unit 6 Lessons 1, 4
2.NBT.2	Count within 1000; skip-count by 2s, 5s, 10s, and 100s.	Unit 1 Lesson 6; Unit 2 Lessons 1, 2, 3, 12, 15; Unit 4 Lesson 15; Unit 5 Lesson 2; Unit 6 Lessons 1, 4 **Daily Routines:** Money Routine; Comparing 2-Digit Numbers; Dimes, Nickels, Pennies **Quick Practices:** Count by 2s, Count by 10s to 120, Count by 10s from 130 to 240, Count by 1s from 1 to 50, Count by 1s from 51 to 100, Count by 1s from 100 to 150, Count by 1s from 150 to 200, Count by 5s from 5 to 100, Count by 5s from 100 to 200, Count by 10s to 200, Count by 100s to 1,000
2.NBT.3	Read and write numbers to 1000 using base-ten numerals, number names, and expanded form.	Unit 2 Lessons 1, 2, 3, 4, 5; Unit 6 Lessons 1, 2, 4 **Daily Routines:** Money Routine, Comparing 2-Digit Numbers, Comparing 3-Digit Numbers **Quick Practices:** Teen Machine; Unscramble the Hundreds, Tens, and Ones
2.NBT.4	Compare two three-digit numbers based on meanings of the hundreds, tens, and ones digits, using >, =, and < symbols to record the results of comparisons.	Unit 2 Lessons 5, 15; Unit 3 Lesson 6; Unit 5 Lesson 10; Unit 6 Lessons 3, 15 **Daily Routines:** Comparing 2-Digit Numbers, Comparing 3-Digit Numbers

Use place value understanding and properties of operations to add and subtract.

2.NBT.5	Fluently add and subtract within 100 using strategies based on place value, properties of operations, and/or the relationship between addition and subtraction.	Unit 1 Lessons 9, 16; Unit 2 Lessons 2, 4, 13, 14, 15; Unit 3 Lesson 9; Unit 4 Lessons 3, 4, 5, 6, 11, 12, 13, 14, 15, 17, 18, 19, 20, 21, 22, 23; Unit 5 Lessons 5, 7, 8; Unit 6 Lessons 3, 8, 10, 15; Unit 7 Lessons 4, 5 **Daily Routines:** Money Routine, Math Mountains for 100 or 2-Digit **Quick Practice:** Quick check

2.NBT.6	Add up to four two-digit numbers using strategies based on place value and properties of operations.	Unit 1 Lesson 9; Unit 2 Lessons 6, 8, 9, 10, 14; Unit 4 Lessons 14, 15; Unit 7 Lessons 4, 5
2.NBT.7	Add and subtract within 1000, using concrete models or drawings and strategies based on place value, properties of operations, and/or the relationship between addition and subtraction; relate the strategy to a written method. Understand that in adding or subtracting three-digit numbers, one adds or subtracts hundreds and hundreds, tens and tens, ones and ones; and sometimes it is necessary to compose or decompose tens or hundreds.	Unit 2 Lessons 4, 6, 7, 8, 9, 10, 11, 14, 15; Unit 4 Lessons 1, 2, 3, 5, 6, 7, 8, 9, 10, 12, 13, 15, 16, 17, 23; Unit 6 Lessons 2, 5, 6, 7, 8, 9, 10, 11, 12, 13, 14, 15 **Daily Routine:** Money Routine **Quick Practice:** Add Over the Hundred
2.NBT.7.1	Use estimation strategies to make reasonable estimates in problem solving.	Unit 4 Lesson 14; Unit 6 Lesson 12
2.NBT.8	Mentally add 10 or 100 to a given number 100–900, and mentally subtract 10 or 100 from a given number 100–900.	Unit 2 Lesson 4; Unit 6 Lessons 2, 4 **Quick Practices:** Trios, Add or Subtract 100, Add or Subtract 10
2.NBT. 9	Explain why addition and subtraction strategies work, using place value and the properties of operations.	Unit 1 Lessons 1, 3, 9; Unit 2 Lessons 2, 4, 6, 7, 8, 9, 10; Unit 4 Lessons 3, 4, 5, 6, 7, 8, 9, 10, 12, 14, 15, 16, 17, 18; Unit 6 Lessons 2, 5, 6, 7, 8, 9, 10, 11, 12, 13, 15 **Daily Routine:** Money Routine **Quick Practice:** Make-a-Ten Cards: Addition; Make-a-Ten Cards: Subtraction

2.MD Measurement and Data

Measure and estimate lengths in standard units.

2.MD.1	Measure the length of an object by selecting and using appropriate tools such as rulers, yardsticks, meter sticks, and measuring tapes.	Unit 3 Lessons 1, 2, 3, 4, 6, 7, 8, 9; Unit 4 Lesson 23; Unit 7 Lesson 1
2.MD.2	Measure the length of an object twice, using length units of different lengths for the two measurements; describe how the two measurements relate to the size of the unit chosen.	Unit 3 Lessons 7, 8, 9
2.MD.3	Estimate lengths using units of inches, feet, centimeters, and meters.	Unit 3 Lessons 3, 4, 6, 7, 8; Unit 4 Lesson 23 **Daily Routine:** Estimating Units of Length
2.MD.4	Measure to determine how much longer one object is than another, expressing the length difference in terms of a standard length unit.	Unit 3 Lessons 1, 2, 6; Unit 4 Lesson 23

Relate addition and subtraction to length.

2.MD.5	Use addition and subtraction within 100 to solve word problems involving lengths that are given in the same units, e.g., by using drawings (such as drawings of rulers) and equations with a symbol for the unknown number to represent the problem.	Unit 4 Lesson 23; Unit 7 Lessons 3, 4, 5

2.MD.6	Represent whole numbers as lengths from 0 on a number line diagram with equally spaced points corresponding to the numbers 0, 1, 2, . . ., and represent whole-number sums and differences within 100 on a number line diagram.	Unit 7 Lessons 3, 5 **Daily Routine:** Comparing 2-Digit Numbers

Work with time and money.

2.MD.7	Tell and write time from analog and digital clocks to the nearest five minutes, using a.m. and p.m. Know relationships of time (e.g., minutes in an hour, days in a month, weeks in a year).	Unit 5 Lessons 1, 2 **Daily Routine:** Time
2.MD.8	Solve word problems involving combinations of dollar bills, quarters, dimes, nickels, and pennies, using $ and ¢ symbols appropriately. Example: *If you have 2 dimes and 3 pennies, how many cents do you have?*	Unit 2 Lessons 11, 12, 15; Unit 4 Lessons 1, 2, 10, 15; Unit 6 Lesson 1 **Daily Routines:** Money Routine; Dimes, Nickels, Pennies; Math Mountains for 100 or 2-Digit Numbers

Represent and interpret data.

2.MD.9	Generate measurement data by measuring lengths of several objects to the nearest whole unit, or by making repeated measurements of the same object. Show the measurements by making a line plot, where the horizontal scale is marked off in whole-number units.	Unit 3 Lessons 6, 7, 8
2.MD.10	Draw a picture graph and a bar graph (with single-unit scale) to represent a data set with up to four categories. Solve simple put-together, take-apart, and compare problems using information presented in a bar graph.	Unit 5 Lessons 3, 4, 5, 6, 7, 8, 9, 10

2.G Geometry

Reason with shapes and their attributes.

2.G.1	Recognize and draw shapes having specified attributes, such as a given number of angles or a given number of equal faces. Identify triangles, quadrilaterals, pentagons, hexagons, and cubes.	Unit 3 Lessons 2, 3, 4, 5, 9; Unit 7 Lessons 1, 2, 4
2.G.2	Partition a rectangle into rows and columns of same-size squares and count to find the total number of them.	Unit 7 Lessons 1, 6
2.G.3	Partition circles and rectangles into two, three, or four equal shares, describe the shares using the words halves, thirds, half of, a third of, etc., and describe the whole as two halves, three thirds, four fourths. Recognize that equal shares of identical wholes need not have the same shape.	Unit 5 Lesson 2; Unit 7 Lessons 1, 2, 6

California Common Core Standards for Mathematical Practice

MP.1 Make sense of problems and persevere in solving them.

Mathematically proficient students start by explaining to themselves the meaning of a problem and looking for entry points to its solution. They analyze givens, constraints, relationships, and goals. They make conjectures about the form and meaning of the solution and plan a solution pathway rather than simply jumping into a solution attempt. They consider analogous problems, and try special cases and simpler forms of the original problem in order to gain insight into its solution. They monitor and evaluate their progress and change course if necessary. Older students might, depending on the context of the problem, transform algebraic expressions or change the viewing window on their graphing calculator to get the information they need. Mathematically proficient students can explain correspondences between equations, verbal descriptions, tables, and graphs or draw diagrams of important features and relationships, graph data, and search for regularity or trends. Younger students might rely on using concrete objects or pictures to help conceptualize and solve a problem. Mathematically proficient students check their answers to problems using a different method, and they continually ask themselves, "Does this make sense?" They can understand the approaches of others to solving complex problems and identify correspondences between different approaches.

Unit 1 Lessons 2, 4, 6, 7, 9, 10, 11, 12, 13, 14, 15, 16, 17, 18, 19, 20, 21

Unit 2 Lessons 1, 2, 3, 4, 5, 6, 7, 8, 9, 11, 12, 13, 14, 15

Unit 3 Lessons 1, 3, 6, 9

Unit 4 Lessons 1, 2, 3, 4, 5, 6, 7, 8, 9, 10, 11, 12, 13, 14, 16, 17, 18, 19, 20, 21, 22, 23

Unit 5 Lessons 1, 3, 4, 5, 6, 7, 8, 9, 10

Unit 6 Lessons 1, 4, 5, 8, 9, 10, 11, 12, 14, 15

Unit 7 Lessons 1, 2, 3, 4, 5, 6

MP.2 Reason abstractly and quantitatively.

Mathematically proficient students make sense of quantities and their relationships in problem situations. They bring two complementary abilities to bear on problems involving quantitative relationships: the ability to *decontextualize*—to abstract a given situation and represent it symbolically and manipulate the representing symbols as if they have a life of their own, without necessarily attending to their referents—and the ability to *contextualize*, to pause as needed during the manipulation process in order to probe into the referents for the symbols involved. Quantitative reasoning entails habits of creating a coherent representation of the problem at hand considering the units involved attending to the meaning of quantities, not just how to compute them and knowing and flexibly using different properties of operations and objects.

Unit 1 Lessons 1, 5, 7, 8, 9, 10, 11, 14, 21

Unit 2 Lessons 1, 3, 4, 5, 6, 7, 8, 9, 11, 12, 13, 14, 15

Unit 3 Lessons 1, 2, 3, 7, 8, 9

Unit 4 Lessons 1, 2, 3, 4, 5, 6, 7, 8, 9, 10, 11, 12, 13, 14, 15, 17, 19, 20, 22, 23

Unit 5 Lessons 1, 2, 5, 10

Unit 6 Lessons 1, 2, 4, 10, 12, 15

Unit 7 Lessons 1, 2, 3, 4, 5, 6

MP.3 Construct viable arguments and critique the reasoning of others.

Mathematically proficient students understand and use stated assumptions, definitions, and previously established results in constructing arguments. They make conjectures and build a logical progression of statements to explore the truth of their conjectures. They are able to analyze situations by breaking them into cases, and can recognize and use counterexamples. They justify their conclusions, communicate them to others, and respond to the arguments of others. They reason inductively about data, making plausible arguments that take into account the context from which the data arose. Mathematically proficient students are also able to compare the effectiveness of two plausible arguments, distinguish correct logic or reasoning from that which is flawed, and—if there is a flaw in an argument—explain what it is. Elementary students can construct arguments using concrete referents such as objects, drawings, diagrams, and actions. Such arguments can make sense and be correct, even though they are not generalized or made formal until later grades. Later, students learn to determine domains to which an argument applies. Students at all grades can listen or read the arguments of others, decide whether they make sense, and ask useful questions to clarify or improve the arguments.

Unit 1 Lessons 1, 3, 4, 6, 7, 8, 9, 10, 11, 12, 13, 14, 15, 16, 17, 18, 19, 20, 21

Unit 2 Lessons 2, 3, 4, 5, 6, 7, 8, 9, 10, 12, 13, 14, 15

Unit 3 Lessons 1, 2, 3, 4, 5, 6, 7, 8, 9

Unit 4 Lessons 1, 2, 3, 4, 5, 6, 7, 8, 9, 10, 11, 12, 13, 14, 15, 16, 17, 18, 19, 20, 21, 22, 23

Unit 5 Lessons 1, 2, 3, 4, 5, 6, 7, 8, 9, 10

Unit 6 Lessons 1, 2, 3, 4, 5, 6, 7, 8, 9, 10, 11, 12, 13, 14, 15

Unit 7 Lessons 1, 2, 3, 4, 5, 6

MP.4 Model with mathematics.

Mathematically proficient students can apply the mathematics they know to solve problems arising in everyday life, society, and the workplace. In early grades, this might be as simple as writing an addition equation to describe a situation. In middle grades, a student might apply proportional reasoning to plan a school event or analyze a problem in the community. By high school, a student might use geometry to solve a design problem or use a function to describe how one quantity of interest depends on another. Mathematically proficient students who can apply what they know are comfortable making assumptions and approximations to simplify a complicated situation, realizing that these may need revision later. They are able to identify important quantities in a practical situation and map their relationships using such tools as diagrams, two-way tables, graphs, flowcharts and formulas. They can analyze those relationships mathematically to draw conclusions. They routinely interpret their mathematical results in the context of the situation and reflect on whether the results make sense, possibly improving the model if it has not served its purpose.

Unit 1 Lessons 10, 11, 12, 13, 15, 16, 17, 18, 19, 20, 21

Unit 2 Lessons 4, 6, 7, 11, 12, 14, 15

Unit 3 Lessons 6, 7, 8, 9

Unit 4 Lessons 3, 4, 5, 7, 10, 12, 13, 18, 19, 20, 21, 23

Unit 5 Lessons 3, 5, 8, 9, 10

Unit 6 Lessons 9, 11, 14, 15

Unit 7 Lessons 3, 6

MP.5 Use appropriate tools strategically.

Mathematically proficient students consider the available tools when solving a mathematical problem. These tools might include pencil and paper, concrete models, a ruler, a protractor, a calculator, a spreadsheet, a computer algebra system, a statistical package, or dynamic geometry software. Proficient students are sufficiently familiar with tools appropriate for their grade or course to make sound decisions about when each of these tools might be helpful, recognizing both the insight to be gained and their limitations. For example, mathematically proficient high school students analyze graphs of functions and solutions generated using a graphing calculator. They detect possible errors by strategically using estimation and other mathematical knowledge. When making mathematical models, they know that technology can enable them to visualize the results of varying assumptions, explore consequences, and compare predictions with data. Mathematically proficient students at various grade levels are able to identify relevant external mathematical resources, such as digital content located on a website, and use them to pose or solve problems. They are able to use technological tools to explore and deepen their understanding of concepts.

Unit 1 Lessons 3, 4, 6, 20, 21

Unit 2 Lessons 1, 2, 3, 4, 5, 8, 12, 13, 14, 15

Unit 3 Lessons 1, 2, 3, 5, 6, 7, 8, 9

Unit 4 Lessons 1, 2, 3, 4, 7, 8, 9, 11, 15, 18, 23

Unit 5 Lessons 1, 2, 5, 10

Unit 6 Lessons 1, 2, 5, 7, 10, 15

Unit 7 Lessons 1, 2, 3, 6

MP.6 Attend to precision.

Mathematically proficient students try to communicate precisely to others. They try to use clear definitions in discussion with others and in their own reasoning. They state the meaning of the symbols they choose, including using the equal sign consistently and appropriately. They are careful about specifying units of measure, and labeling axes to clarify the correspondence with quantities in a problem. They calculate accurately and efficiently, express numerical answers with a degree of precision appropriate for the problem context. In the elementary grades, students give carefully formulated explanations to each other. By the time they reach high school they have learned to examine claims and make explicit use of definitions.

Unit 1 Lessons 1, 2, 3, 4, 5, 6, 7, 8, 9, 10, 11, 12, 13, 14, 15, 16, 17, 18, 19, 20, 21

Unit 2 Lessons 1, 2, 3, 4, 5, 6, 7, 8, 9, 10, 11, 12, 13, 14, 15

Unit 3 Lessons 1, 2, 3, 4, 5, 6, 7, 8, 9

Unit 4 Lessons 1, 2, 3, 4, 5, 6, 7, 8, 9, 10, 11, 12, 13, 14, 15, 16, 17, 18, 19, 20, 21, 22, 23

Unit 5 Lessons 1, 2, 3, 4, 5, 6, 7, 8, 9, 10

Unit 6 Lessons 1, 2, 3, 4, 5, 6, 7, 8, 9, 10, 11, 12, 13, 14, 15

Unit 7 Lessons 1, 2, 3, 4, 5, 6

MP.7 Look for and make use of structure.

Mathematically proficient students look closely to discern a pattern or structure. Young students, for example, might notice that three and seven more is the same amount as seven and three more, or they may sort a collection of shapes according to how many sides the shapes have. Later, students will see 7×8 equals the well remembered $7 \times 5 + 7 \times 3$, in preparation for learning about the distributive property. In the expression $x^2 + 9x + 14$, older students can see the 14 as 2×7 and the 9 as $2 + 7$. They recognize the significance of an existing line in a geometric figure and can use the strategy of drawing an auxiliary line for solving problems. They also can step back for an overview and shift perspective. They can see complicated things, such as some algebraic expressions, as single objects or as being composed of several objects. For example, they can see $5 - 3(x - y)^2$ as 5 minus a positive number times a square and use that to realize that its value cannot be more than 5 for any real numbers x and y.

Unit 1 Lessons 1, 2, 5, 6, 9, 13, 17, 18, 19, 21

Unit 2 Lessons 1, 2, 3, 4, 6, 10, 11, 12, 15

Unit 3 Lessons 1, 3, 4, 5, 6, 7, 8, 9

Unit 4 Lessons 1, 2, 7, 13, 17, 19, 21, 23

Unit 5 Lessons 2, 6, 7, 10

Unit 6 Lessons 4, 12, 13, 15

Unit 7 Lessons 2, 6

MP.8 Look for and express regularity in repeated reasoning.

Mathematically proficient students notice if calculations are repeated, and look both for general methods and for shortcuts. Upper elementary students might notice when dividing 25 by 11 that they are repeating the same calculations over and over again, and conclude they have a repeating decimal. By paying attention to the calculation of slope as they repeatedly check whether points are on the line through $(1, 2)$ with slope 3, middle school students might abstract the equation $(y - 2)/(x - 1) = 3$. Noticing the regularity in the way terms cancel when expanding $(x - 1)(x + 1)$, $(x - 1)$ $(x^2 + x + 1)$, and $(x - 1)(x^3 + x^2 + x + 1)$ might lead them to the general formula for the sum of a geometric series. As they work to solve a problem, mathematically proficient students maintain oversight of the process, while attending to the details. They continually evaluate the reasonableness of their intermediate results.

Unit 1 Lessons 2, 6, 7, 21

Unit 2 Lessons 5, 10, 11, 15

Unit 3 Lessons 1, 2, 7, 8, 9

Unit 4 Lessons 4, 8, 13, 23

Unit 5 Lessons 2, 10

Unit 6 Lessons 2, 4, 7, 8, 12, 15

Unit 7 Lessons 1, 2, 6

Index

Index (continued)

B

C

© Houghton Mifflin Harcourt Publishing Company

H

I

L

M

Index (continued)

Index (continued)

Q

R

S

© Houghton Mifflin Harcourt Publishing Company

Index (continued)

is greater than (>), 83–84, 267–268

is less than (<), 83–84, 267–268

right angle, 121

unknown (□), 24

T

Take From Word Problems. *See* Problem Types.

Tape diagrams. *See* Comparison bars.

Three-dimensional figures. *See* Geometry.

Time

a.m./p.m., 224, 232

analog/digital clock, 223–225, 227–228

calendar, 233–234

half-hour, 230

hour hand, 223, 228

minute hand, 223, 228, 230–231

minutes in an hour, 229, 233

to five minutes, 230–234

to the hour, 227–228

unit relationships, 233

Triangle, 123, 127–128, 132

Two-dimensional figure. *See* Geometry.

Two-step problems. *See* Problem Types.

U

Ungroup 100, 169

Ungroup Challenge, 187–188

Ungroup First Method. *See* Algorithms; Subtraction.

Ungrouping. *See* Algorithms; Subtraction.

Unit Review and Test, 67–70, 111–114, 155–158, 217–220, 255–258, 299–302, 329–332

Unknown addends or partners, 15–16, 38, 44

addition, 199–200, 203–204, 207

count on, 169

Math Mountains, 159–160

subtraction, 169, 207, 326

word problems, 199–202, 281

V

Vertical form. *See* Equations.

Visual thinking. *See* Spatial Reasoning.

W

What's the Error?, 18, 23, 60, 79, 84, 92, 93–94, 168, 176, 210, 231–232, 245, 248, 267–268, 326. *See also* Puzzled Penguin.

Word problems, 3, 5, 31–44, 49–60, 65–66, 77–78, 81, 90, 169, 182, 189–190, 195–196, 199–204, 207–209, 212, 213–214, 272, 275, 281, 285, 293–298, 315–317, 323–325. *See also* Problem Solving; Problem Types.

estimate answers, 196, 290

© Houghton Mifflin Harcourt Publishing Company

Index (continued)